HOW FREE ARE YOU?

HOW FREE ARE YOU?

The Determinism Problem

Second Edition

TED HONDERICH

OXFORD
UNIVERSITY PRESS

OXFORD
UNIVERSITY PRESS

Great Clarendon Street, Oxford OX2 6DP

Oxford University Press is a department of the University of Oxford.
It furthers the University's objective of excellence in research, scholarship,
and education by publishing worldwide in

Oxford New York

Auckland Bangkok Buenos Aires Cape Town Chennai
Dar es Salaam Delhi Hong Kong Istanbul Karachi Kolkata
Kuala Lumpur Madrid Melbourne Mexico City Mumbai Nairobi
São Paulo Shanghai Singapore Taipei Tokyo Toronto

with an associated company in Berlin

Oxford is a registered trade mark of Oxford University Press
in the UK and in certain other countries

Published in the United States
by Oxford University Press Inc., New York

© Ted Honderich 2002

The moral rights of the author have been asserted
Database right Oxford University Press (maker)

First published 2002

British Library Cataloguing in Publication Data

Data available

Library of Congress Cataloging in Publication Data

Data available

ISBN 0–19–925197–5

10 9 8 7 6 5 4 3 2 1

Typeset in Dante
by RefineCatch Limited, Bungay, Suffolk
Printed in Great Britain by
T.J. International Ltd., Padstow, Cornwall

To Ingrid

Acknowledgements

Since this is a book, it must contain obscurities and mistakes. There are fewer of them because of suggestions made by Richard Double, James Garvey, Anthony Grayling, Angela Griffin, Scott Hagan, Germund Hesslow, Basil Hiley, John Honderich, Kevin Magill, Paul Noordhof, Jane O'Grady, Ingrid Coggin Purkiss, Sarah Richmond, Michael Scott, Galen Strawson, Ruediger Vaas, Pat Walsh, and Roy Weatherford. My warm thanks to them.

Contents

1

INTRODUCTION TO TWO SUSPECT THEORIES

THIS book is about a problem that will get a hold on you. It will, anyway, if philosophers past and present are any guide. The greatest of them, as well as the not-so-great, have struggled with it. Some have been upset by it, some have sided with predecessors, some have tried to reduce it to science, some have announced brazen solutions. The problem is determinism. That is, the question of whether your choosing this book and your reading this sentence now, or your deciding to move in with someone or get divorced, is just a matter of cause and effect.

There are so-called theories that come to nothing much, or anyway not enough. Some of them are outside of ordinary science and philosophy and outside of the universities, but a lot of them are inside. For example, there are philosophical theories by scientists, some of them about the subject of consciousness, that as philosophy seem hardly worth the paper they're printed on.

Theories may be talked and written about, taken on trust, have a great success. They may even last. But they are not clear, consistent, and worked-out. In short, they aren't conceptually adequate. When you really try to get a hold on them, they turn out to be obscure, or they do not hang together, or they are undeveloped. They are failures even *before* you try to test them to see if they're true.

Is the theory of determinism like that?

It has been around long enough, and most of us have some idea of what it is. Its supposed upshot is that we are not free in anything we choose or do, and aren't to be held morally responsible for our actions or given moral credit for them. Determinism presumably goes against the special idea or kind of freedom that is still called Free Will. That is something we do feel we've got, and would be alarmed to lose. If we find ourselves in front of a judge, we may be told firmly that we had Free Will when we chose to commit the offence. He may not use the archaic term, but we will get the idea anyway.

Chapters 2–5 of this book try to deal with the suspicion that determinism, even if it has been around for a long time, is not a conceptually respectable theory—not explicit, consistent, and complete. In short, that determinism doesn't add up to a real philosophy of mind and action. More than one philosopher has said so. It has often been implied by scientists—maybe not just because they tend to get befuddled by a kind of thinking clearer than their own.[1]

These chapters, in particular chapter 4, also have to do with the contrary idea of Free Will.[2] According to this idea, each of us has a kind of personal power to *originate* choices and decisions and thus actions. Their coming-about or initiation definitely wasn't just a matter of cause and effect. Thus on a given occasion, with the past just as it was and the present and ourselves just as they are, we can choose or decide the opposite of what we actually do choose or decide. We can go on to act differently from the way we actually do.

There is reason for as much or more suspicion about *this* theory. Is *it* respectable? Does it give us what deserves the name of being a philosophy of mind and action? Is it made respectable by what it usually includes, an interpretation of the troubled part of physics that is Quantum Theory?

To get these opening chapters into better view, a couple of distinctions are needed. The term 'determinism' is used in different ways by philosophers and others. It is traditionally used as the name of a very general theory about all of reality, including the non-living world and in particular the small particles of physics.

---

[1]   Science has the great strength of being more empirical than philosophy, closer to the small facts of the world. As a result, it can give less attention to conceptual adequacy—to *logic* in a large sense. We need both science and philosophy.

[2]   The term 'free will' can also be used more loosely to mean, as it seems, our freedom generally—where that may be understood as including something very different from origination. As remarked and in short, this other thing is our not being frustrated. Perhaps the wide or umbrella use of 'free will' is intended in the title *The Oxford Handbook of Free Will*. I shall use the term in the more precise sense, but continue to write it as Free Will in order to indicate that sense.

Sometimes this general theory is contemplated or worked out in terms of mathematical equations. It then amounts to determinism in terms of physics.

But determinism is also ordinarily taken as an idea, doctrine, or theory about persons, one that is non-mathematical and includes in itself the proposition that somehow we aren't free and responsible. We have a certain nature or human nature and as a result of this we aren't free and responsible.

A third use is along the same lines as the second but different. Here, determinism is only a view of our nature—in essence, the view that ordinary causation is true of us and our lives, that in our choosing and deciding we are subject to causal laws. In this use of the word, determinism comes to no more than a yes answer to the question of whether we are in one fundamental way like plants or machines. Determinism in this sense does not include or imply an answer to the question of whether we are free or not. That question, maybe surprisingly, is left pretty well untouched.

There is a reason for this third, restricted understanding.

There has been a strong tradition in philosophy that maintains that we are or we may be subject to ordinary causation—but we can be free anyway. If we examine our concept of freedom we learn that we can be free in the ordinary way, the only way that matters. In a word, this has to do with not being frustrated. We can therefore be held responsible for our actions or given credit for them given that they were not contrary to our desires. This ordinary freedom and responsibility does not have to do with Free Will at all. Being subject to causation is logically compatible with what we all mean by being free if we don't get confused. There is no contradiction.

This 'Compatibilist' tradition, as you might expect, has been denied. Indeed there has been another strong tradition in philosophy that is mainly concerned to deny Compatibilism. What is maintained in the 'Incompatibilist' tradition is that logically you can't be both determined and really free. You *can't* have it both ways. In the real sense of the word, you can't be free if your decisions and actions are just a matter of cause and effect. If you get our concept of freedom straight, there *is* a contradiction. You therefore can't be held responsible or given moral credit for an action in the way that you could be if it wasn't an effect but was in another way owed to you.

None of this will be very clear yet, but what may be clear is that it is a good idea to try, as best we can, to separate two entangled questions. One is the question of whether we persons are subject to causation or instead have a different nature. Using the third, restricted sense of the word 'determinism', as I always will from now on, this is the question of determinism. The other question, as it is usually put, is about what *follows* if determinism is true. Does it follow logically that we are not free? That is the question of the consequences or implications of determinism. It is the problem to which philosophers have given most attention.

So—the opening chapters look into the conceptual respectability of determinism, and also of an indeterminist philosophy of mind and action. That is, one that denies that our nature is as much a matter of causation as plants and machines, and in virtue of this is indeterminist, but also credits us with the personal power of *origination*. This power may be assigned, more precisely, to a self or originator within a person. Like determinism, in this day and age, all this will also have to fit the brain into its story, try to accommodate the large fact of neuroscience.

Such a philosophy of mind and action, by the way, despite the distinction between the question of determinism and indeterminism and the separable question of implications for freedom, can also be called a philosophy of Free Will. Given our chosen definition of determinism, the usage is annoying, but it is hard to resist, and I myself may lapse into speaking in this way. But the fact of language doesn't mean there aren't two more or less separable questions. One is about our natures, and one is about whether or how we are free. If you want, I guess, you could also say that one question looks straight at the facts of our natures, and the other looks at the facts in terms of their implications, say for moral responsibility.[3]

---

[3]   All this can be puzzling and confusing. One reason is that supposed facts of our human nature—origination—*are* the facts of our freedom according to one tradition of thought. (This is the main reason why the annoying usage exists.) And other supposed facts of our nature, not yet explained but having to do with our desires not being frustrated, *are* the facts of our freedom according to the other tradition of thought. But the first lot of supposed facts, according to the *second* tradition, are *not* the facts of our freedom. And the second lot of facts, according to the *first* tradition, are *not* the facts of our freedom. So clearly it is a good idea to separate two questions.

Chapters 6 and 7 face the obvious next question after that of the conceptual respectability of determinism, which in fact isn't the question about freedom. As already implied, a theory can be clear, consistent, complete—and false. There may be one to the effect that the earth is flat. There is certainly an economic one to the effect that privatizing publicly owned organizations, say railways or water boards, lowers prices and is good for us. What we want, of course, are *true* theories, or as close as we can get to them. If it turns out that both determinism and indeterminism have the three intellectual virtues that have been mentioned, can we come to a judgement about which one has the crowning virtue? Which one is *true*?

Chapters 8–11 *do* deal with the question of the consequences or implications of determinism, and hence the doctrines of Compatibilism and Incompatibilism. The same question of consequences, by the way, is raised by something perhaps more widely accepted than determinism. That is *near-determinism*. Maybe it should have been called *determinism-where-it-matters*. It allows that there is or may be some indeterminism but only at what is called the micro-level of our existence, the level of the small particles of our bodies, particles of the kind studied by physics. At the ordinary level of choices and actions, and even ordinary electrochemical activity in our brains, causal laws govern what happens. It's all cause and effect in what you might call real life.

The question is whether if determinism, or near-determinism, is true, it follows that we are not free and responsible. It has been a philosophical battleground for centuries. There have been great philosophers on both sides. David Hume (1711–76), the finest of philosophical thinkers in the English language, was a redoubtable Compatibilist. To jump from the eighteenth to the twentieth century, Jean-Paul Sartre (1905–80), the French Existentialist, was an Incompatibilist. Immanuel Kant (1724–1804), perhaps the greatest of German philosophers, was an Incompatibilist too, although of a unique kind.

Might it be that both sides are wrong, in more than one way?

When they think about determinism affecting our freedom, might they be wrong in their conception of the kinds of consequence of determinism, in their view of the number and the nature of those consequences? Is the worry or threat of determinism really mainly about one thing, moral responsibility, as almost all Compatibilists and almost all their opponents seem to have supposed? Or mainly moral responsibility and the attached question of the justification of punishment? Morality plays a large part in our lives but, rightly or wrongly, it is far from being everything.

There is a second question. Might both sides also be wrong in thinking that we really get hold of the fundamental problem, wherever it arises, just by asking, however we are advised to go about it, whether 'determined' and 'free' are logically consistent terms, whether both can be true of the same thing? Like 'round' and 'green' as against 'round' and 'square'? Is our question of the consequences of determinism such a purely intellectual question about our concept of freedom? One where yet another 'proof' will settle things? There have been a lot of 'proofs', some aided by kinds of formal or symbolic logic. And it's certainly true that determinism and our holding people responsible and the like has a lot to do with our attitudes, feelings, and, indeed, desires.

Might both Compatibilists and Incompatibilists be wrong in a third way, still more fundamentally? Might they be wrong in believing that one side or the other in their battle has got to be right? Might they be wrong in believing that one side or the other must have hold of the truth about the bearing of determinism on other things, however few or many of those things there are? It's easy to be inclined to agree with that belief of theirs. You will want to say either that determinism is consistent with freedom or that it isn't. One of those *has* to be true. Just as it *has* to be true that either you're over six feet tall or you're not.

I think Compatibilists and Incompatibilists are wrong in all three ways. It turns out that they can be. More people agree with this unorthodoxy than used to. It's not as unorthodox as it was. Conferences of philosophers on determinism and freedom aren't the same as they used to be.

So this book is both an introduction to a great problem and an argument. It both reports on and participates in a discussion. It is for the general reader. It is also for lawyers, doctors, scientists, physicists in particular, psychiatrists, criminologists, theologians, psychoanalysts, and all others who find themselves faced with or attracted to the great problem. But first of all it is for the hurried student of philosophy. That does not make it a hurried book, as another writer of introductions genially if competitively inferred (McFee). It does need to be admitted, or maybe promised, that it is a kind of précis of the 644 pages of my *A Theory of Determinism: The Mind, Neuroscience, and Life-Hopes*. It follows the same path.

But this second edition is different in many places, and it doesn't stop with just the same conclusion. I've had some second thoughts—hence chapter 12. So it goes further than its large predecessor and also than the first edition of itself.[4] It starts along another line of enquiry. It leaves both of us, writer and reader, with a new thing to think about. It could be that it is better in this way.

It definitely is better than its large predecessor in other ways. It's shorter. It's up-to-date and has a substantial bibliography.[5] It also has a glossary of philosophical terms at the end, which may be useful already. What exactly was that thing called origination? How are indeterminism, Incompatibilism, and Free Will related?

---

[4]   There are also lesser differences between this second edition of *How Free Are You?* and the first. This edition updates the first edition as well as its large predecessors, and should be a little clearer throughout.

[5]   Proper names in brackets are those of authors of writings listed in the bibliography at the end of the book. When necessary, to distinguish between different writings by the same author, the names are followed by the year of publication. Philosophers named in the ordinary way in the main text also have their relevant writings listed in the bibliography.

2

REAL AND OTHER EFFECTS

THE subject of effects has had attention throughout the whole history of philosophy and has divided great philosophers. Is it a little dull anyway? Don't be too sure. In any case it is the best place to start in trying to decide whether determinism is a respectable theory. In its central part, determinism *is* the theory that our choices and decisions and whatever other events give rise to them are effects.

It is best understood as taking them to be effects in the ordinary rather than in any special sense—effects as we ordinarily speak of them. One reason for doing so is that we can then look at the question of determinism's truth directly by way of our ordinary knowledge of effects. We won't have to try to translate our knowledge into other terms.

What the theory comes to, then, will depend on what we actually take effects to be. That is our question. Of course, asking about an effect brings in our idea of a cause. This is so because effects and causes are each partly defined in terms of the other. Still, it is effects that are fundamental to the subject of determinism and how it affects our lives. Rightly or wrongly, most of us are not too worried by talk of our choices having causes. Can't a free choice have a cause? But we may be worried by our choices being effects, or, as some say ominously, *just* effects. That idea does carry a chill.

The chill will not stay on us, by the way, if it turns out that what we take to be an effect is just an event that was *probable* given the fact that some previous event happened, as some philosophers have contemplated (Eells; Mellor). No doubt your reading this sentence as this moment makes it probable that you will read the next one.

But that fact of probability, with no more said about it, doesn't seem to imply that you won't be reading on freely.

To amplify a little, if determinism turns out to be just the theory that it is probable beforehand that all our choices and hence our actions will happen as they do, then the theory will indeed not trouble us much. Even if we take the theory to be a plain truth, that will not really disturb our conviction that we freely choose things, that we are responsible for our actions, and so on. Nor, on reflection, may there be much change in this situation if effects are taken to be very highly probable events. If an event is 99 per cent probable, or 99.99 per cent probable, that can leave it open to us to make the difference as to whether it actually happens or not. It leaves it up to us finally.

In fact, far from giving us a determinism, the idea of effects as merely probable events goes into the opposite doctrines— indeterminism and Free Will. Some advocates of these doctrines explain that at least part of what is meant by saying that choices, decisions, and actions are originated is that they are caused or are effects in the sense of being probable (Kane 1996). Very rightly, the advocates of Free Will see no danger to their conclusion in talking of these funny effects in order to start making sense of origination.

But to try to stick to our official subject, which is not yet determinism's chill and doctrines of Free Will, but just what ordinary effects are, they definitely aren't just probable events. Nor, even, are they just events with a probability of 1—that is, 100 per cent certain. That an event has a probability of 100 per cent given some preceding event is not the same fact as the fact that it somehow *has to happen*. Ordinary effects do somehow *have to happen* as a result of what precedes them. It isn't just that they do happen. The necessity of them is the hallmark of ordinary effects, as you can easily come to see.

Probability is a difficult and much disputed subject (Benenson; L.J. Cohen; Weatherford), but suppose things change dramatically in our lives and we can actually see into the future. We don't know at all how we do it—no idea—but we do do it. We see events happening next year. So aren't they now 100 per cent probable? But that won't necessarily make them into *effects* as we understand them, will it? We now know that they will happen but not that they will be caused to happen. Couldn't one of them be an action of mine, 100 per cent probable but still perfectly free in any sense at all that you can think of, and therefore not an effect?

So much for the idea of effects as just probable.[1] Here is what may be a related idea, though. Is an ordinary effect just an event that something else had the *power* to produce? Well, we won't get our real idea of an effect, which has a definiteness about it, if this talk of a power to produce something is left as vague as it often is.

And, incidentally, I don't have to become apprehensive about whether I am responsible for my decisions if I have the thought that something has this power to produce them. Maybe a thing's having such a power doesn't mean that it has got to produce some decisions rather than others. Maybe the thing was just 'enough' for the result, where that puzzlingly doesn't mean the result had to occur. It just happened to occur (Anscombe; Kenny). Also, this thing with the power might just be *me*, which seems reassuring. And finally, there won't be any trouble in allowing in the same vague way that something else had the power to shape this me.

But forget about responsibility and all that, and come back again to our official subject. Do we think that the ordinary effect of the hen's egg on the marble floor being hit with the heavy hammer was something that happened to happen, but didn't have to? Hardly anybody is so keen to save our Free Will as to say so. If we don't have a special agenda, what do we really suppose effects to be? Take the lighting of a match here and now. When we assume that this event was the effect of the match's being struck, what are we assuming? Something about the effect's having to happen, certainly, but what?

If you start thinking not about that particular point but in a general way about effects, one first idea is the plain one that the lighting of the match was an event that wouldn't have happened if the match hadn't been struck. On the assumption that the striking was cause and the lighting was effect, what is true is that *if the first hadn't happened, neither would the second*. That is true, at any rate, if the situation was an ordinary one. In an extraordinary situation where a match was struck in a curious place, i.e. *within* the flame of another match, the striking wouldn't have been required for the lighting. The match would have lit anyway.

We are reluctant to say something else about an ordinary striking

---

[1]   But see pp. 52–3 in Chapter 4 for a little more on the subject.

and lighting—at least at first. We are reluctant to say that *if or since the first thing happened, so did the second.* The explanation of our reluctance is that even if the match was struck, had it been wet, it wouldn't have lit.

There is at least a problem about this reluctance. We are supposing that we shouldn't say that since it was struck, it lit—because more had to be true than that it was struck. It had to be dry. But go back to what we took as unproblematic, that if it hadn't been struck, it wouldn't have lit. Presumably we shouldn't say that either—because more had to be true than that it wasn't struck. One thing that had to be true is that it wasn't held in the flame of another match. Or is it that we can rightly say both things? If it hadn't been struck it wouldn't have lit, and since it was struck, it lit? That's my idea, but let me skip the details.[2]

There are more puzzles about causes and effects, where those are events typified by a striking and a lighting. Many of these puzzles can be intriguing, but we need not attend to them. What needs to be taken forward with us in our enquiry, despite the puzzles, is the fact that causation seems to be a matter of relations between things. How things in the world have to go together. These are relations which we are inclined to describe by way of such conditional statements as the ones we have noticed—if the match hadn't been struck, it wouldn't have lit, and since the match was struck, it lit.

That isn't to say, by the way, that causation is a matter of language or anything of the sort. Causal relations are not things in the world in the sense that the match is a thing, but they are certainly facts of the world. Conditional statements are true of reality, just as the non-conditional statement that there are matches is true of reality. Causation seems to be no more in the mind than matches (cf. Cartwright).

It has to be said that it has become popular to analyse causal relations in terms of what are called *possible worlds*. In place of saying that if the match hadn't been struck, it wouldn't have lit, something is said along these lines: in a possible world where the

---

[2] Almost everything passed over in this book, up to near the end, is made more explicit in *A Theory of Determinism: The Mind, Neuroscience, and Life-Hopes,* reprinted in the two paperbacks *Mind and Brain* and *The Consequences of Determinism.* But the further detail isn't necessary to a perfectly good understanding of this book.

match wasn't struck, or in the possible world in some sense most like ours, it didn't light. And it is said that the possible world, which is not ours, is as real as ours (Lewis). My own view, and that of most philosophers, is that causal relations are real things in the only world that there is. Also, to speak for myself and a good many other philosophers, the technicality of possible-worlds talk when it is bound up in a kind of formal logic, while engrossing to some, does not make causation any clearer at all.

We will get to the heart of the matter of effects, in so far as determinism is concerned, by thinking of something other than the relation between a cause and its effect. We will get to the heart by thinking of the relation between (1) a set of things that included the cause and (2) the effect. One such set of things was in view when it was noticed that not only the striking was required for the lighting, but also the match's being dry. And that was not all that was required. There had to be oxygen present, and the surface on which the match was struck had to be of a certain kind.

What is the difference between a cause and the set of things that included it, which set of things we can call a *causal circumstance*? It could also be called a total cause, by the way. Or a sufficient cause, although the latter term has several uses.

Suppose that we do a little science and come to the conclusion that the causal circumstance for the lighting, by one way of describing it, had five parts to it, one being the striking of the match. Suppose too that a second match is now about to be struck. It seems dry and so on—we are confident that in a moment there will exist counterparts of all of the five parts of the original circumstance—so all that remains is the striking. But when this set of counterparts seems to have been made complete, by someone's actually striking the second match, the match doesn't light. What do we think?

We have one of two thoughts. The first is that in fact, despite our confidence, we did not really have a circumstance including the five parts. Maybe the match was a little wet. Or we think that the bit of science we did after the first lighting was inadequate. There was a five-part circumstance when the second match didn't light. But what was true earlier when the first match did light was that there existed a *six*-part circumstance. We missed one part of it in our attempt at science.

What is common to both of these thoughts is that a causal

circumstance for an effect is something such that *all* counterparts of the circumstance are followed by like effects. We do not think that a true causal circumstance for an effect could have been something such that a counterpart circumstance would not be followed by a like effect. To put it differently, we do not think that exactly one type of causal circumstance goes with different types of events—that sometimes it goes with an effect and sometimes it doesn't.

What can be taken to follow from this is an answer to the question of the difference between a cause and the circumstance of which it was part. An event that caused a certain effect is not necessarily such that all like events are followed by like effects. Not all strikings are followed by lightings. A causal circumstance for a certain effect, on the other hand, really is such that all like circumstances are followed by like effects.

The next idea is that what makes something a causal circumstance is no more than this fact—this is our whole idea of a causal circumstance. The idea is owed to David Hume. In his language, what makes something a causal circumstance for something else is that the two things are an instance of a constant conjunction. What that comes to is that every thing like the first is followed by or conjoined with a thing like the second.

It's an idea lovely for its simplicity, but it cannot be the whole story. While it does indeed seem true that each causal circumstance and effect is such that each like circumstance has a like event following it, that is not all that is true. One of Hume's critics in the eighteenth century, Thomas Reid, provided the most famous example to show this—a day and a night.

Consider yesterday, which we specify as just a certain period of light on a certain surface of the earth. Consider last night, which we specify as just a certain period of darkness on the same surface of the earth. All things like the first, which is to say other days, are followed by things like the second, other nights. But yesterday was not the causal circumstance for last night. It certainly would be if a causal circumstance and its effect were no more than an instance of a constant conjunction.

We can get to the fundamental truth about causation by considering this famous example further. We have a good idea of what the causal circumstance for last night really was. It included the earth's relevant surface being turned away from the sun, the absence of any alternative light source, and the behaviour of light. Light from the sun doesn't bend round the curvature of the earth to light up the far side. Let us call this true causal circumstance for last night the solar conditions.

We now have two pairs of items: yesterday and last night, and the solar conditions and last night. What is the difference between them? If we can see that, we can see what makes the second pair a causal circumstance and its effect.

Well, it seems to be a fact that yesterday might have happened, just as it did, without being followed by last night. Without anything's having been subtracted from yesterday, we might not have got last night. This would have been the case, for example, if a great new light source had come into existence in the right place when yesterday ended. If the universe had changed in certain ways, ways consistent with the occurrence of yesterday, we would not have got last night.

What about the other pair, the solar conditions and last night? It seems that however the universe had changed, consistent with the continued existence of the solar conditions, last night would still have happened. That is the difference between our two pairs.

The main conclusion of our enquiry into the nature of effects is that we take an effect to be an event that was preceded by a causal circumstance—such a circumstance being something that would still have been followed by the effect whatever else had been happening. If we understand by 'X' any possible change in things consistent with the existence of a causal circumstance, then what was true of the circumstance is that since it occurred, even if X had occurred, the effect would still have occurred. Nothing else mattered or could have got in the way.

This fits our ordinary ways of thinking and talking of effects. As remarked several times already, we think that when certain things are a certain way, what we call an effect has to happen or must happen. It couldn't fail to happen. Effects are in a way necessary or inevitable, and nothing else could happen instead of them. To use a philosophical term I shall stick with, effects are *necessitated* events, events necessitated by their causal circumstances.

According to the conclusion we have come to, what is said in all these and other ways is mainly that given a causal circumstance, whatever else had been the case, the effect would still have occurred. A necessitated event is one for which there was a circumstance that was such that since it occurred, whatever else had been true, the event would still have occurred (cf. Sosa and Tooley).

The conclusion we have could be expressed differently—in terms of talk of possible worlds, or mathematically in terms of equations, but there is no need at all for that. Some philosophers and scientists have a tendency to intrude their specialities on large ideas and problems, but not often with real gain. If our aim is philosophical progress, we need not join them. Our conclusion about causation, however, *does* need defending against certain objections. And, as a preparation for the defending, we need to notice some things about it.

One is that any single causal circumstance has in it just enough to guarantee the effect, no more than that. It doesn't have any redundant parts. That will be of some importance later. Another thing is that the causal circumstance for an effect will typically be made up of parts that were also effects themselves. So, as we can say, this whole circumstance was the effect of an earlier one, maybe a long time before. Then the earlier circumstance also necessitated the final effect. This fact about effects—the fact of what you might call causal chains—is very important to determinism.

Another matter has to do with natural or scientific laws. It is usually supposed, for good reason, that an effect involves such a law. Philosophers have sometimes supposed that an effect is to be defined as an event that follows other events as a matter of natural or scientific law. They say that in general an effect is something such that from certain premises it follows logically that it occurs. The premises are certain statements of fact about the world—e.g. that a match is dry—and certain statements of law or lawlike statements. But then these philosophers face the problem of completing their job by giving an account of natural laws. They are likely to find themselves talking in a general way about the relations stated by conditional statements (cf. Hooker; Armstrong).

The conclusion we have is in a way simpler, and contains in itself an analysis of laws. It involves the idea that for two things to be connected by a natural law just *is* for them to be such that if the first happens then, whatever else is happening, the second also happens.

To introduce another term, let us say that if two things were connected in this 'whatever-else' way, they were in *nomic* or lawlike connection. Are causal circumstances and effects the only things that are in this kind of connection? They won't be if we make definite a certain step we have already taken unofficially.

We have been thinking of causal circumstances as coming before their effects in time. We did not have to do that. There is room for decision here. Let us now take the official decision that what we will count as causal circumstances do indeed precede their effects. In that case we evidently have room for pairs of things that are nomically connected but are not causal circumstances and effects. They are simultaneous in time. They can be called nomic correlates. Science provides quite a number of examples. One is a matter of properties of a gas, say temperature and pressure, that go together. Another example has to do with the two stars that make up a double star. Looking forward, do brain and mind provide another?

Another thing to be noticed about the conclusion to which we have come, although ways of expressing it can be misleading, is that it is about our conception or idea of an effect. It is not itself a conclusion about the way the world is, about reality. We have not come to the conclusion that we ourselves are a matter of cause and effect, perhaps that all mental events are effects. Of course, some people deny that, but they can nevertheless agree with what has been concluded. That is, they can agree that anything that really is an effect is an event necessitated in the given way. Of course, the fact that we take effects to be necessitated events is pretty good evidence that at least some events in the world are such events. Where else would we get the idea?

The last thing to be noticed before turning to the objections is a qualification or caveat. It seems that we are not perfectly consistent in our talk about what we call effects. When we have in mind broken eggs, lightings of matches, and nights, and indeed all events other than our own choices and decisions, we speak of effects and mean necessitated events. But do you say that your decision to buy this pink shirt rather than that blue one, or vote for this political party rather than that, was an effect of something or other, or at any rate had this or that cause—but yet was not a necessitated event?

You may be inclined to say that, and, if we now took time to think about it, you might change your mind. That is, you might change your mind about what you really have in your mind on the subject of the causation of choices and decisions. But let us pass by that subject. Let us simply say that what we have been and are concerned with in our reflections here is *standard* effects—all so-called effects except choices and decisions and the like. These standard effects, we say, are necessitated events. We are very interested indeed, of course, in whether choices and decisions, however we talk of them as effects, are in fact also standard effects and therefore necessitated. But that is another matter, ahead of us.

Now to the first of three objections to our conclusion that effects are necessitated events—events standing in the described relation to a previous circumstance, and very likely to a predecessor of that circumstance. It is an objection that is alive and well today but it got its clearest form a while ago from a very clear-headed philosopher (Mackie).

An ordinary gambling machine, otherwise known as a fruit machine or one-armed bandit, is designed in such a way that when you put in a coin, a causal mechanism operates, and you do or do not get coins out, a pay-out. The whole thing, as we say, is deterministic. Now think of an imaginable machine which its owners might be unwise to have. In place of a causal mechanism inside, it has a mystery-mechanism that gives rise to truly unpredictable events. Whether a little switch flips or not, with the result that coins come out or not, is truly unpredictable. More plainly, there is no causal circumstance for the switch's flipping when it does, and no causal circumstance for its not flipping when it doesn't. If you don't put a coin in, you can't win, but winning or losing is a matter of real chance.

Some say that when you put in a coin, and do get a pay-out, the later event was the effect of the earlier one. They ask what else could it be? They then draw the general conclusion that what we take to be a standard effect is not a necessitated event but *merely an event preceded by something that was required for it*. An effect is just a later thing such that if something earlier hadn't happened, the later thing wouldn't have happened either. Maybe they are a little motivated to think this by the idea that it will help out later with showing that we have Free Will. But that doesn't matter now. Are they right in their conclusion?

It seems to me that they aren't. You put a coin into the special machine and fortunately the switch flips. There is something very special about the flipping, which we must not overlook. The flipping is an event that has no explanation. I don't mean merely that we don't know the explanation, but that there is none to know. To say the same thing differently, the question 'Why did it happen?' is not just a question to which we don't know the answer. There is no answer that it has. There is no answer that God, if he existed, could find.

This becomes clear when one remembers that, according to the story, the machine and the world could have been exactly the same, up to the moment when the switch flipped, and still it might not have flipped. Between this history in which the switch flipped, and the possible history in which it didn't, there is *nothing* that could explain what actually happened. There is *no difference*. Everything that is in this history could have been in the possible history without the switch's flipping. To speak differently again, the flipping is a mystery.

If this is what is true of the flipping, it certainly wasn't an effect. (For reasons you have heard about, it doesn't become one, either, if it was probable, even very probable.) An effect, since something else made it happen, is precisely something that *has* an explanation. It is precisely something that is *not* a mystery. To go back to what was said initially about the special machine, that it involves chance events, an effect is precisely something that is *not* a chance event. But if your putting in the coin wasn't linked to your pay-out by a chain of causes and effects, which we see it wasn't, how could the last event be the effect of the first? How could the pay-out be the effect of putting in the coin?

We can speculate why some people think it could be. Of course the pay-out was *an* effect. It was the effect of the switch's flipping. No doubt the flipping was part of a causal circumstance for the pay-out. It is just as true that your putting in a coin was *a* cause, and no doubt part of a causal circumstance. But that was the causal circumstance whose effect was just the turning-on or starting-up of the mystery-mechanism. What we haven't got is the pay-out being the effect of putting in the coin. We haven't got the conclusion that an effect is just something preceded by something that was required for it. It seems to be just a confusion to think we have an effect of something that is not a causal circumstance.

Here is another kind of objection to our conclusion that we take effects to be necessitated events. Think about what we actually believe when we assume something was an effect. There is marmalade on the kitchen floor. We believe this came about because Jane dropped the jar. We also believe that when it slipped from her fingers she just might have caught it with the other hand. Some say on the basis of such examples that we take effects to be things that happen as a result of something, so long as nothing gets in the way. That 'something', since another thing can get in the way of it, evidently isn't a causal circumstance (cf. Mackie).

Let us call what usually results in an event, according to this story, a 'usual cause'. Then the view being urged on us is that *an effect is what follows on a usual cause*, where a usual cause is certainly not what we have been calling a causal circumstance.

What are we to think of this view? It's true that we do often have in mind usual causes. Indeed usual causes are what we almost always have in mind with respect to effects. Science itself is for the most part concerned with usual causes. That is all very well, but would we take something to be an effect if we believed it had only a usual cause and was not the result of a causal circumstance?

We need to keep the right question clearly in mind. We are not asking whether something was an effect if it had a usual cause *and* that usual cause was really part of what also existed, a causal circumstance. That such an event was an effect is in perfect accordance with our own conclusion that effects are necessitated events. What we are asking is whether the marmalade on the kitchen floor, say, would be an effect if there was the usual cause of the jar slipping from Jane's fingers, but nothing that necessitated the unhappy result.

Well, if that really were true, there would be no explanation of the marmalade on the floor. Just as in the case of the flipping of the switch in the fruit machine, the event would be a mystery. There cannot be any explanation of it since everything you might contemplate as an explanation could have been just the same without the spilt marmalade. The situation is just the same as with the fruit machine. So the split marmalade wasn't an effect. In general, then, effects aren't merely events that follow on usual causes. We can persist in our conclusion that they come from causal circumstances.

We might think some more about all this, which has puzzling features, but consider instead the last objection. It is really a bundle of objections, some of which go back to the early works of Bertrand Russell.

It may not have escaped your notice that we have got this far without actually specifying a causal circumstance—enumerating all its parts without exception and giving a good account of each one. We did not go far in the case of the circumstance for the lighting of the match, or the solar conditions in connection with last night, or the circumstances with the fruit machine and the spilt marmalade.

Such facts have led some to imply that we do not even have a clear idea of a causal circumstance. That is just a bad argument. To leave aside causation, I do not at the moment have a complete and detailed description of *all the man-made things in this room*. But that is not to say that I do not have a clear idea of what falls under that description. General ideas aren't necessarily unclear (cf. Lucas, 1962).

An objector would do better to begin by saying that if effects are what we have supposed them to be, then to confirm or verify that something is an effect of a certain kind, we must have a complete and detailed description of a causal circumstance. How else can we test a belief that something was the effect of something in particular? In fact, the objection continues, each of us has a multitude of such beliefs, rightly and confidently held. But we do not have anything like a multitude of complete and detailed descriptions of causal circumstances. It must be then that our causal beliefs do not in fact involve the idea of a causal circumstance.

This sort of thing has impressed some philosophers, but does it really stand up? What we have a multitude of, even if we are practising scientists, for instance neuroscientists, is not beliefs that something was owed to a fully known causal circumstance. We have beliefs that something is necessitated *in part* by something else. Striking the match causes it to light. We have beliefs that some state of affairs *somehow includes* what necessitates some event. These beliefs definitely rest on the supposition of the existence of causal circumstances, but do not require complete and detailed descriptions of them.

There is one other related line of objection. Sometimes we do have what can be called full explanations of the occurrence of events. There are some of these in science, if not nearly so many as is sometimes supposed. But, according to this last and most tough-minded objection, we *never* have a complete and full description of what has been called a causal circumstance. We can never get hold of something such that once it happened, no matter what else was the case, we would still have got the upshot. To have that we might have to specify the whole state of the universe, maybe the whole history of the universe up to the moment of the event. So something has gone wrong.

The main thing to be said about this is that it involves forgetting what a causal circumstance is. Such a thing is not *all* of what was required for something. If the universe began with a big bang that resulted in oxygen's coming into existence for the first time, then that big bang was indeed something required for the house fire. But we can certainly give a causal circumstance for the fire without going into all of that. A causal circumstance is what is just enough to necessitate an effect, and there was one of those just before the fire, inside the house.

So much for what we take effects to be. If we think our lives *are a* matter of effects, we think they are a matter of events that really have to happen because of earlier causal circumstances, not events that are anything less than that. But can our idea of effects be used to give a persuasive picture of our choices and actions, and above all their coming-about or initiation? Can it be used in a persuasive philosophy of mind and action? That comes next.

3

MIND AND BRAIN

How are minds connected to brains? Or, to ask a question that will do as well and seems clearer, how are mental events, events of consciousness, connected to neural events? How is your awareness now of the place you're in, or your thinking in reading this sentence, related to what is going on in the grey stuff of your brain? If you choose to stop reading now and do something else, maybe your duty, how is the choosing related to what is going on in your brain?

The question of the mind–brain connection is often taken as the fundamental one in the philosophy of mind. An industry of philosophers, psychologists, and cognitive scientists are engaged in examining, rejecting, propounding, and being confused by answers to the question (Warner and Szubka; Priest). It must also be one question at the centre of determinism and freedom.

In answering it, everything—or anyway an awful lot—turns on what we take being aware of or thinking something or choosing something to be. To speak generally, what *are* mental events? What is the nature of consciousness? This really is the fundamental question in the philosophy of mind. What are these items that make up what are called the streams of our conscious lives and which we can distinguish or mark off in them? We need to answer this prior question before, or anyway in the first stage of, answering the question of how mental events are related to neural events. This prior matter must be quite as much at the centre of determinism and freedom.

As you might expect, an answer to the question of the nature of conscious events may actually settle or go a long way towards dealing with the question of how conscious events are related to the electrical and chemical events in the brain. The opposite is also true, of course. You can give an answer to the relationship question that settles the nature question. This can be the case, depending on what you actually mean, if you say the relation of mental events to neural events is just that mental events *are* neural events—they are *identical* with or *just the same things as* certain neural events.

To take an extreme example of settling the relationship question by answering the nature question, a couple of Californian philosophers have seemed to take a view of the nature of mental events that boils down to this: mental events are nothing, in a way less than nothing (P. Churchland; P. M. Churchland). This is not the view or rather the views just mentioned, that mental events are identical with certain neural events, to which we will certainly come.

Rather, it is the view that mental events are just a confusion—our ordinary talk of mental events in terms of beliefs, desires, choices, and various other categories, otherwise known as our folk psychology, is a confusion that needs to be eliminated. We need to restrict ourselves to categories and ideas of neuroscientists that apply only to the brain. If that were true, we could in fact forget about the question of the connection between mental events and neural events. There wouldn't be one, or at least there wouldn't be any remotely interesting one.

The question of the nature of mental events is not quite the same as the question of what the mind is. It is certainly simplifying, and somehow right, to take a mind as just being a stream or sequence of mental events. But it is possible to try to have an idea of a mind that is not just an idea of this stream. We can try to think of a mind as a private place or space in which mental events occur. We can also try to think of a mind as an inner something for which mental events exist, or an inner thing to which mental events happen or for which they happen. In the latter case some go as far as speaking unhesitatingly of the mind as a subject—or a self, ego, or even a soul.

It seems that the ultimate true answer to the question of what mental events are may *somehow* have to respect at least the impulse we have to think of the mind as a place or subject. It is not as if we can ignore that feeling or image, and declare that our minds just consist in sequences of mental events, where those events are conceived without reference to the feeling or image. It seems too that philosophers do not respect these images of unity enough when they ask if a sequence of mental events involves one locale or thing only in the vanishingly small sense that many of the events in it are rememberings of earlier ones or anticipations of later ones (Parfit).

I will not try to suggest a full answer to the question of the nature of mental events, but only beginnings of an answer, or some necessary moves towards an answer. The first thing to say is that mental events, despite their elusiveness and mysteriousness, are *real*. We do all believe this, for good reason, and what does it amount to? Well, presumably that they are as much in time and space as anything else.

There seems relatively little difficulty about their being in time, and also about their lasting for a time, however short. We can say when a mental event occurred with about as much confidence as we can say, for example, when the candle was lit or went out. There is more difficulty about regarding mental events as being in space. But why is that?

The answer seems to be that they typically involve what can be called contents, although the term can also be used differently. We have the thought *that* such-and-such, maybe the thought that there is a line of trees out of the window. *That there are trees out of the window* seems not to be here or in any other place. What are called propositions, like numbers, are not in space. But are such contents *parts* of mental events? It is only if they are really parts that their not being in space will also subtract mental events from space, at least partly.

There are arguments for thinking that such contents are not parts of mental events. One is that if they were, mental events would not be in time either. This is so because contents aren't in time. It isn't just space that they are missing from. *That there are trees out of the window* is not now, or at any other time. *That Fountain House dates from 1818* isn't then or now or at any other time. But mental events *are* in time. We are sure enough of that. So contents can't be part of them.

If this argument does not satisfy you, here is another one. Apart from the occasional philosophers mentioned earlier who are rightly said to try to eliminate the mind as a confusion, everyone agrees that mental events are real. You could not give a full description of what exists and leave them out. But what can believing they are real come to if it does not come to believing, among other things, that they are in space and time? Anyone who allows they are real, or that they exist, and also says they are not spatio-temporal, owes us an explanation of what he or she is saying. What is this funny kind of existence? Until an explanation is given, it seems that he or she doesn't have a position to defend.

Do you have the feeling that a little too much attention has now been given by me to the matter of the reality of mental events? That their reality is obvious? Well, as was said in passing, we *also* take them to be elusive and mysterious. In this situation, and in connection with determinism, it is worth going on about their reality. Determinism can seem less than it is, maybe less persuasive—and the opposing doctrines less than they are, maybe less strange—if you half think that conscious events are just some kind of gossamer.

There is a second thing to be said of mental events, quite as important. Their great distinctiveness is that they are *subjective*. They have a certain subjective nature or character. The word 'subjective' is put to a lot of uses, in and out of philosophy, but maybe this is the fundamental one. There is a difference between my existence and the existence of a chair, which is that my existence has this subjective side—or, as you might say, *inside*. That is somehow true, but what does it actually come to? It sometimes seems there are as many answers as there are philosophers of mind.

We ourselves can get the subjectivity of a mental event into view. We can recollect or retrospect the nature or character of a mental event just past. If there has been a lot of scepticism about introspection, our having a kind of inner eye to turn on our own consciousness, we can certainly ask ourselves, perfectly sensibly, about what it was to be conscious a moment ago, what that mental event was.

Shall we say that in itself it involved two related things, *something's existing for something else*? When I thought there are trees out of the window, wasn't there something that existed for something else? What existed for something else wasn't the trees, since I might have had the thought without the trees, without there being any trees. It also seems that what existed for something else could not have occurred on its own, not in relation to the other item, not for the other item. It seems too that I cannot think of this other item as having nothing existing for it—as not being in this relation to anything. So shall we say that mental events have about them what we can call an interdependent duality (Honderich 1994b)?

This is vague, and does little more than report the images we have which issue in larger and more doubtful doctrines. In these we get the subject, self, ego, soul, or some other entity than a person but also named by *I*, put in place of what was called the other item, and also this entity's activities, possessions, or properties. But it is better to be vague than to fail entirely to get hold in language of something that we know about.

So—mental events are in space and time and they have a discernible character or nature, their subjectivity. As for neural events, which are less baffling, we can say for the moment that they involve only membranes and other small structures in the brain, electrical impulses, chemical transmitter substances such as acetycholine, parts and regions of the brain and central nervous system, and so on. Neural events, in short, have only electrochemical properties. They only have the properties of the bodily cells in question, neurons, the stuff of neuroscience.

To come to the question of how mental events are related to neural events, many answers in this day and age try to fit in with three ideas. In fact they are only misleadingly called ideas, since almost all of us are convinced of them. The first one is the idea of *psychoneural intimacy*. What it comes to is that there is some extremely close connection between a mental event and an associated neural event. There is some kind or other of necessary connection. The idea is partly owed to the discovery in neuroscience that particular types of mental event somehow go together with types of events in particular parts of the brain, and that this is certainly no accident.

The second idea is that mental events themselves do affect what we do. Put differently, the mental event of my wanting a glass of wine, like the mental event of my seeing the bottle on the sideboard, is itself part of the explanation of my stepping over to get one. That seems truistic. In the nineteenth century, there were Epiphenomenalists—thinkers convinced that mental events are by-products of neural events, and not themselves part of the explanation of actions. There are not many Epiphenomenalists left, at least in philosophy. I think there is one in Australia (Jackson).

The third idea or conviction is also about the explanation of actions. It comes from common sense, and more importantly from neuroscience. It is just that *neural* events are also explanatory of actions. Even a little knowledge of the motor cortex of the brain makes that hard to resist—in fact, impossible.

What account of the relation between mental and neural events would satisfy these three ideas—that mental and neural events are intimately related, that mental events somehow explain actions, and that neural events also somehow explain actions? An obvious line to take, anticipated above, is to *identify* a mental event with a neural event, say they are *one thing*. This has seemed obvious to many. It promises to give us psychoneural intimacy, and also make both the mental and the neural explanatory of actions. There is also the promise of a *very* simple determinism.

Many have tried to take the obvious line, or, as it turns out, one or the other of two lines. What is meant by saying a mental event *was* or *was identical with* a neural event? The answer, to cut a long story short, has to be that the mental event had all and only the properties of the neural event. If this is the case, it seems we have to ask any Identity Theorist what properties he takes the mental event to have had. To this question, he has two possible answers, which lead to two different kinds of theories.

His first possibility is a kind of single-mindedness. In this single-mindedness he *could* say, but in this day and age isn't likely to, that the mental event had only mental properties. It only had properties that are a matter of its subjectivity. But if he says this, he is committed to saying that the neural event had only such properties. It didn't have electrochemical properties as we understand them at all—nothing of an electrical impulse going down the axon of a cell and the like. You could say he is in the bizarre position of mentalizing or spiritualizing the brain. He joins or is on the way to joining the very rare breed of metaphysicians who are panpsychists (Sprigge).

The Identity Theorist, in this day and age, if he is single-minded, is almost certain to say something else in answer to the question of what properties he takes the mental event to have. He will in effect say it had only neural properties, only electrochemical properties (Papineau; Honderich 2001c). That answer is uncomfortable, to say the least. So the Identity Theorist then is likely to try to coat the pill of what is in fact the materialism about the mind that went with the rise of science in the seventeenth century.

One coating of the pill is Functionalism, and a related one is Cognitive Science of a philosophical kind (Block; Shoemaker;

Lycan). The central thing said by the proponents of these doctrines is that what makes an event mental is not its being a neural thing in me or a silicon thing in a computer but just its *relations* to other things, its causal or its logical relations. The idea owes something to but gets miles away from the truism that one thing about a desire, say, is likely to be that it is the result of seeing something and the cause of an action.

Functionalism and philosophical Cognitive Science, at this point in time, as the new millennium gets under way, are popular doctrines among philosophers and theoreticians of the mind. They are as popular as was their predecessor, Behaviourism, which at its most batty was the idea that your consciousness, maybe your feeling of love for your child, is only your limb movements and other such purely bodily behaviour. Functionalism and philosophical Cognitive Science seem to me to face difficulties that are just as insuperable.

The first one is that when they say that my wanting to see Ingrid this morning is an event in my head with certain relations, they don't thereby make my wanting significantly more than a neural event. The coating doesn't change the pill. This is still just the old materialism, and it will never succeed against our cast-iron conviction that consciousness isn't cells (Honderich 1994a).

Certainly, if these doctrines were true, there could be no problem at all about stating a clear determinism. It would be simple. Our central subject-matter would be reduced to no more than brain events. That is what decisions and choices and all of consciousness would be. So determinism would simply be the theory, truistic to many, that brain events are effects. There would be no problem about fitting in a relationship between brain events and something different, the decisions and choices that go with them. But none of us can really believe that consciousness is just cells.

So go back to where we were. The Identity Theorist, when he identifies a mental event with a neural event, and we ask him what properties he takes the mental event to have, should say something different. He shouldn't be so single-minded. His other possibility is to say that it had properties of subjectivity and also electrochemical properties. Some contemporary Identity Theorists do go this way (Davidson 1980). What in effect they mean, when they speak of identifying the mental and the neural event, is that there was one event that had two kinds of property.

Should we side with them? It depends on what else they say.

Many of them say that my wanting to see Ingrid, which was mental, is to be regarded as a property of one thing, which thing also had neural properties, *and* it was the neural properties that caused my subsequent action. The last bit is added because of a rash assumption about what neuroscience is supposed to have established.

The last bit also makes it hard to swallow the theory, because it seems to make it Epiphenomenalist. In it, the mental properties aren't doing any work. Certainly, it doesn't follow from the fact that *some* properties of a thing are causal or have a certain effect that other properties of the thing are causal in the same way or have the same effect. It doesn't follow from the fact that the weight of a book is flattening a pea that its colour or shape or smell is also contributing (Honderich 1984b; Davidson 1993).

There seems to be nothing wrong with identifying the mental event with the neural event where that comes to saying that there was one thing that had certain mental properties and also certain neural properties. On reflection this is a pretty unadventurous proposition. For a start it does seem sensible to regard mental and neural events as properties of persons. But identifying the mental and the neural in this way doesn't by itself make the mental properties part of the explanation of actions.

If this Identity Theory doesn't pass the test of giving a real role to the mental, that is not its only problem. It is easy to drift into thinking, when someone talks of a mental event being identical with a simultaneous neural event, that he is making them intimate. It is easy to think that his view passes the test of psychoneural intimacy. But does it? All he has said is that what was mental was a property of what was also neural. That isn't to say very much. The kind of intimacy in question is shared by *any* two properties of a thing—the weight and the smell of something again, or my height and my political outlook. It isn't reassuring that a thing could have one of two 'intimate' properties without the other, or keep one and lose the other.

The requirement of psychoneural intimacy is not as clear as it might be. Still, the Identity Theory we are considering doesn't achieve it with flying colours. There is also its Epiphenomenalism. It seems best to try another sort of picture of the psychoneural relation. There certainly are some. They rest on the idea of nomic or 'whatever-else' connection explained in chapter 1.

To put most of this approach into a sentence, let us say that a mental event and an associated neural event are in some way nomically connected—connected in the 'whatever-else' way—and more particularly that the neural event by itself or together with something else non-mental necessitates the mental event. Or we can talk of mental and neural properties instead of events but say the same thing. There is no harm in talking of these pictures as being kinds of Identity Theory. They aren't any more 'dualistic' than the Identity Theory that we have lately been looking at. But there is no need either. What they come to is better suggested by another name. Let us say they are theories of *Mind–Brain Determinism*.

One theory of Mind–Brain Determinism, anticipated in our enquiry into causation (p. 16), can serve as an example. It is the Union Theory, in part that neural events and simultaneous mental events are not causes and effects, but are nomic correlates. This certainly makes for psychoneural intimacy. In more detail, it was true of a certain neural event that since it happened, whatever else had been happening, I would at the same time still have wanted to see Ingrid just as I did. The neural event itself necessitated or guaranteed the mental one. It's also true that if the mental event hadn't happened, neither would the neural. That last bit is reassuring. Mental events are important. They're not just passengers on a brain-bus.

But the theory isn't innocuous. There is what you may take to be a sting in the tail. The first thing we concluded about a causal circumstance for an effect is that *all* like circumstances are followed by like effects. Similarly, if something is a certain kind of neural correlate for something else, then all things like the first are accompanied by things like the second. Call my neural event N and my mental event of wanting to see Ingrid M. Since N was a certain kind of nomic correlate of M, something else is true. If there is ever a counterpart of N in me or anybody else, there will also be a counterpart of M.

Mind–Brain Determinism theories give a general answer to the question of how mind is related to brain, or, more precisely, how associated mental and neural events really are related—they are in a kind of nomic connection. It will turn out that Mind–Brain Determinism theories are one third of a full or complete determinism.

The other two parts have in them theories of how associated mental and neural events come about or what initiates them, and of how subsequent actions come about.

For want of better names, we will call these theories of *Initiation Determinism* and *Action Determinism*. Action Determinism will have to do with the ideas that both mental and neural events are explanatory of our actions (pp. 26–7). Initiation Determinism, about the explanation of mental events, is more fundamental. It is the next item on the agenda. Before turning to it, however, let us pause a little to look at an objection or two to Mind–Brain Determinism. There is no interesting philosophical view that does not face objections, and the worth of a view is importantly owed to what can be said in reply to the objections.

There are objections to Mind–Brain Determinism that seem to boil down to this: consciousness is so different from brain cells and anything else non-conscious that they cannot be in lawlike connection—mental events are so unlike neural events that 'whatever-else' connections cannot hold between them. It may be said that we think of the two sorts of things in terms of very different principles—having to do with physical quantities on the one hand and rationality on the other—and so they can't be in lawlike connection (Davidson 1980). But *why* can't different things be in lawlike connection? We need an explicit reason. Lots of causes are different from their effects. For a small start, a stick of dynamite is a lot less colourful than an explosion.

There are other more explicit and seemingly commonsensical objections to Mind–Brain Determinism. To take an example that may strike a chord with you, one is about a kind of individualism. Consider the example of the Union Theory again. As you have already heard, it has the upshot that if certain identical neural events were to occur in your brain and mine we would be having identical thoughts or feelings—really identical mental events would occur. Aren't persons more individual than that? Neuroscience is a fact, and we can well believe that brains and minds are connected, but why should my mind be connected to my brain in just the way that your mind is connected to your brain (Thorp)?

To go back to the earlier illustration, couldn't it be the case that in my life N and any identical neural events go with wanting to see Ingrid just as I did, but in your life any neural event identical to N would go with some slightly or entirely different mental event?

This alternative view isn't what would be a pretty surprising one, that there is *no* nomic connection between brains and minds. In some way it allows nomic connection. Shall we then take it that it allows that there is nomic connection between just an *N*-like neural event and *something or other* mental? If we do, the view doesn't make much sense. As we have understood nomic connection, it just can't happen that an *N*-like neural event in whoever's head isn't accompanied by the same mental thing. That is ruled out.

This conclusion doesn't depend on exactly the understanding we have of nomic connections. There are other understandings, and they all give us the same conclusion. Take the very simplest one, Hume's. For him, what is true if *N* were a kind of nomic correlate of *M* is just that all events like *N* are accompanied by events like *M*. So no *N*-like event has a different mental companion.

Can we take the individualism objection differently? We might speculate that our personal development is something as follows. Perhaps at an early moment in your life you were aware of something, say a spaniel, and in your head there happened to be occurring a certain neural event, *N1*. In my case, when an identical neural event occurred, I was aware of a bathtub.

That somewhat mysterious speculation might lead to the idea that what goes with a certain present mental event is a neural event and also a past experience. Spaniel thoughts in your case go with neural events like *N1* and a certain past experience, and bathtub thoughts in my case go with the same sort of neural event and a different past experience.

This seems to be another shambles of an objection. Your early spaniel experience isn't flying out of the past and having some kind of direct and unmediated influence on your later thoughts. Nor is my early bathtub experience. What we have to suppose is that there is some ongoing neural fact—*X* in your case and *Y* in mine. But then there is no objection left to the Union Theory. In your case or in anyone's case whenever an *N1+X* neural event occurs, there is a spaniel thought. In my case or anyone else's whenever an *N1+Y* neural event occurs, there is a bathtub thought.

Here is a related objection to the Union Theory. To change the example about my just wanting a glass of wine, suppose I had the thought that *seven o'clock is time for a glass of that Chilean wine*. The thought went with a certain neural event. Now think of a native Canadian in an igloo in the Arctic who has never heard of clock-time or Chile or even wine. Also go in for some wild speculation of a kind urged on us by many philosophers. Imagine that neuroscience has progressed marvellously, if that is the right word, and neuroscientists can now produce neural events to order by stimulating brains electrically.

If the Union Theory is true, they could collect the native Canadian, tell him nothing about the outside world, produce in him just a neural event like mine, and he would think that seven o'clock is the time for a glass of that Chilean wine. That is ridiculous, so the Union Theory is false (cf. Anscombe 1972).

The objection isn't the mistake that the Union Theory or Mind–Brain Determinism theories in general carry any implication whatever about what neuroscientists will in fact come to be able to do. They don't, of course. The objection is that they somehow make something imaginable or coherent or possible to think consistently, when it isn't. But what is it, in general terms, that is unimaginable or whatever?

We are not told that, but we can speculate. In a certain sense, a person can't have a thought in isolation. I might mouth some words, but I can't really have the thought that *it's Tuesday today* if I have no idea of days generally or of time or of a week. To have one thought I have to be able to have many others. This is one thing that might be meant by saying that the mental is *holistic*. It might be a clear thing meant by saying what some do, that thoughts only occur within a form of life.

So it is unimaginable that somebody should have on its own, so to speak, the thought that seven o'clock is the time for a glass of that Chilean wine. That isn't imaginable. *That* is what is ridiculous about the speculation we have gone in for. But, to come to the point, this doesn't help with the objection to the Union Theory. It doesn't claim that there are no conditions that have to be satisfied if someone has the neural correlate of a certain thought. It doesn't say that the neuroscientists would have to do only the little job imagined above.

It remains true that the theory does commit us to thinking that *if* ever there is a repetition of a certain neural event, there is a repetition of a certain mental event. That is not to say that there could be such a repetition in any situation you would like to think of. No doubt there couldn't be a repetition in someone of whom other neural things weren't true—things that go with other mental events.

One more objection to the Union Theory. For various reasons philosophers like to go in for another piece of imagining—a twin-earth. In physical terms it is identical to ours, down to the last detail. There is an identical you on it, physically exactly the same as you. Now suppose two things, that your brain is in a certain state and you have the thought that your girlfriend is in Bognor Regis. Given what has been said, twin-you's brain is in the same state. Is he having the thought that his girlfriend is in Bognor Regis? If the Union Theory is true, he has to be (Putnam; Stich).

The objection is that he isn't having the same thought. He isn't, even if he reports it in exactly the same way and so on. This is so for the reason that your thought is about your girlfriend and twin-you's thought is about somebody else, twin-you's girlfriend. His is also about a different place called Bognor Regis. So the Union Theory is refuted. Identical neural events don't go with identical mental events.

The trouble with this is not really that it involves a doubtful idea of a thought and of mental events generally—although it does. The doubtfulness of it comes out, by the way, when it is noticed that this idea can make two items that are in a fundamental way absolutely identical into two different thoughts. What is perfectly possible is that if you had *both* the mentioned thoughts in the twin-earth story, your thought and then the thought of twin-you, you couldn't discern any difference between them. The same would be true of twin-you if he had both. There could be absolutely no difference between them. They would have exactly the same nature and properties.

As I say, the trouble with the objection isn't that it involves an unusual idea of thoughts that distinguishes between them by what is in the world outside the thinker and not by what they are like to the thinker. The trouble is that the Union Theory *is* about thoughts and so on that are identified by what they are like to their owners. A mental event in terms of the Union Theory *is* something distinguished by its owner and hence by its own nature and properties. The objection says nothing at all about such mental events, and leaves it perfectly possible that they are tied to neural events.

So it is of no importance to the Union Theory that thoughts distinguished in the doubtful way aren't tied to neural events, as of

MIND AND BRAIN   35

course they aren't. Nor does thinking of thoughts and other mental events in the standard way, which is the way of the Union Theory and Mind–Brain Determinism theories generally, leave out anything of our mental lives. The objection thinks of the same subject-matter in a different way—from the point of view of Mind–Brain Determinism, an irrelevant way.

You may be willing to draw the conclusion that some Mind–Brain Determinism theory or other is the most promising theory on offer. Certainly, I myself have that conviction. But a bit of hesitancy is in order. It is very plain that the problems of the nature of consciousness and its relation to the brain are unsolved, or anyway remain in dispute. They are still there after you see that Functionalism and the like don't solve them. You can be confident in propounding your own theory, and still admit that consciousness is a fundamental difficulty in philosophy, and that maybe the true account of it will be *very* different from present stories.

The whole problem of determinism and freedom, as we know, has the problem of consciousness in the middle of it. So, to come to the point, there will also be room for some hesitancy about determinism and freedom. We can go forward thinking about determinism and freedom in terms of Mind–Brain Determinism. But, at the very end of our reflections, we may find ourselves thinking again.

One last thing. Nothing much has been said of how the philosophers of indeterminism and Free Will—the philosophers of origination noted in chapter 1—treat the questions of the nature of consciousness and the relation between conscious events and neural events. That is because hardly any of them have had anything to say in answer to exactly these questions. They have not been in that competitive industry of philosophers, psychologists, and cognitive scientists mentioned earlier, the mainstream of the philosophy of mind and recently the mainstream of philosophy itself.

It is true, as we shall soon be seeing, that the philosophers of indeterminism and Free Will do get in sight of the questions in another way, when they try to explain how conscious events come about. But it is tempting to wonder, given the relevance of the mentioned industry, the mainstream of the philosophy of mind, if the philosophers of indeterminism and Free Will have been a little careless in being off to one side, not in touch. Can they afford to ignore the mind–brain problem and the nature-of-consciousness problem as these are generally considered in philosophy and so on? In particular, would they find their own conclusions harder to arrive at if they were more in touch?

So much now for how mental or conscious events go with neural events. What brings these things about? What initiates them?

4

CAUSATION? ORIGINATION?

THE theory of determinism we are putting together, and more particularly the fundamental part that can be called Initiation Determinism, takes a choice to be a real effect, like the neural event associated with it. The choice is not an uncertain effect of some funny kind. That is important, but it isn't everything. In order to be a real determinism the theory also needs to take the choice to be an effect of some causes rather than others, or, as you might say, *enough* causes. This is easy to see.

Suppose you took the view that someone's choice, say Toby's choice to try to leave his secure job, was a real effect—but of something or other that definitely was not an effect itself. Maybe this thing was the forming of an intention, a forming of an intention to choose as he then did. It was a kind of pre-choice. Whether the pre-choice took place an instant before the fateful choice itself, or a long time before, this view wouldn't be determinism but more or less the opposite.

Shall we say that what Initiation Determinism comes to with respect to a particular choice is that it was an effect and everything that led up to it or was in the story behind it was an effect? Well, that would be something of the right sort, but when you think about it, it is more than a little unclear what led up to a particular choice—what it is for something to lead up to a choice.

We can do better. Let us avoid the difficulty by saying, in a way, that all choices and other conscious events are effects of heredity and environment. To make our theory more explicit we need the idea of a causal sequence or chain. The shortest complete one of these consists in an effect preceded by a causal circumstance and that causal circumstance preceded by a still earlier one for it—for all of it. Most sequences we think about are longer, chains with more links.

Everything *within* any causal sequence, which is to say everything but the parts of the initial causal circumstance and the final effect, whatever may be true of them, is both an effect and a cause. There aren't any gaps. Thus it is true of the sequence that the final effect was made necessary not only by middle or intermediate circumstances but also by what we are calling the initial circumstance. When you get the initial circumstance, the end of any sequence is settled.

Although we are not likely to think of the possibility at first, the parts of a causal circumstance, even an initial causal circumstance, can occur at different times, even very different times. To go back to the lighting of the match, suppose we first describe a causal circumstance for it in terms of the match's being dry, in oxygen, struck, and the surface it is struck on being of the right kind. We take these four things as being at the same time, the time of the striking. But we get another perfectly good causal circumstance if we take the first three items together with something earlier that guaranteed that the surface was of the right kind at the time of striking.

The causal sequence for any choice or any other conscious event, we say, is such that the parts of the initial causal circumstance occur at different times. They are also of different sorts. Some of the earliest parts are neural facts and other bodily facts just prior to the very first mental event in the history of the person in question. The other parts of the initial causal circumstance are events in the person's environment then and thereafter, probably right up to the time of the choice or whatever.

To have a definite idea of these environmental events, we can restrict them to items that affect a person directly, not through intermediaries. So each of these items is the *last* item in some environmental story, presumably causal, and this item's immediate effect is a bodily or neural event of the person in question. Suppose Toby's saying something shirty to his boss makes his boss feel that he may have to take a difficult decision about him. Our initial causal circumstance for his feeling this at the moment doesn't include all of Toby's history leading up to his words, but only the very last bit.

What we arrive at, then, is the idea that each choice and other conscious event is the effect of a causal sequence whose initial circumstance has in it neural and other bodily events just before the first moment of consciousness of the person in question, and what can be called last environmental events then and thereafter.

Certainly, the sequence for almost any choice will be complicated beyond tracing. For a start, there will be a multitude of conscious events *within* the sequence. A lot of them will have to do with learning. There will also be a multitude of things so far unnoticed, mental dispositions. These are dispositions to think or feel this or that, and are best regarded as persisting neural structures. In my view they are what can properly be meant, by the way, by evocative talk of the subconscious or the unconscious mind.

However impossible it is to set out all the links of a single causal sequence, we have a clear idea of what this explanation of the mental event comes to. We don't have to know the details, any more than we have to know the details to understand the claim that what crushed the daisy in the valley was the avalanche that started up on the mountain.

As with Mind–Brain Determinism, it will help to have in mind a particular idea of consciousness and the brain, the Union Theory. What it comes to is that conscious events, events of subjectivity, are nomic correlates of simultaneous neural events (see p. 30). Here is a model or diagram of Initiation Determinism in terms of this theory. Or rather, a model or diagram of a very small part of such an Initiation Determinism.

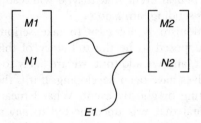

$M1$ is Juliet's mental event, her feeling at a particular moment about having met a man called Toby. It goes with her neural event $N1$. As for $E1$, it is some last environmental event which comes a little later. The event $E1$ together with the pair made up of $M1$ and $N1$ are the two parts of a causal circumstance for what comes later, the pair made up of another mental event $M2$ and another neural event N2. Maybe M2 is a happy feeling of anticipation on Juliet's part. The model leaves out everything before the time when M1 happened, and so doesn't come near to showing the very early neural and bodily events in the long causal sequence.

This is a good moment to glance at something distracting that goes against all of this. It is a picture of the mind which admittedly comes from true things we say. We say some mental events are effects and some are causes. Seeing something is an effect and deciding something is a cause. We also say that some mental events are both effects and causes. These beliefs can in fact be explained in terms of the picture of the mind we have been developing, but some philosophers have done otherwise. They have come up with something called Interactionism (Eccles and Popper). Here is a little model of a version of it.[1]

The first item shown in the model is neural event N1 in Juliet, maybe having to do with the neural side of her seeing or hearing something. N1 causes Juliet's feeling about having met Toby, M1, to happen a moment later. Another moment later, M1 has the effect N2, which is a neural event that maybe will lead to the physical action of Juliet's sending him a note.

This Interactionism is not easy to take seriously, for several reasons. It is supposed to be the full story of this bit of Juliet's history. If it isn't, and we add to it, we are likely to get the sort of thing we ourselves have been developing. If it *is* the full story, M1 was a free-floating or ghostly event. What I mean is that it was something mental that was unconnected to *any* neural event at the moment. That is about as hard to believe in as ghosts themselves, which if they existed would also be free-floating mentality.

---

[1]   The model is of a clear version of interactionism—a deterministic one. Eccles and Popper offer us an indeterministic and obscure one, of which a bit more is said below on p. 46.

Another problem is the explanation of *N2*. That was a neural event which came out of nothing neural. At the moment before *N2*—at the moment of *M1*—there was nothing happening neurally. That is not a promising move in theory-construction, and is hard to swallow. We don't think there are *gaps* in a brain's history, gaps in the history of a part of a physical body. If our present business is setting out and clarifying a theory, whether Initiation Determinism or Interactionism, we can't help but do so with an eye on probable truth.

Interactionism as sketched is a bad determinism, which must not delay us. What really needs attention is the kind of explanation of mental events that is radically different from all of what we have been considering so far. This different kind is in terms of Free Will and is indeterministic, not a matter of causation as we know it. It has often been assumed and talked about, and it has also been set out in full complexity by industrious philosophers. In fact, they say more than anyone is likely to have the fortitude to be able to consider.

A Free Will theory may have a source in religion, now American religion in particular (Ekstrom; Boyle et al.). It may have a source in politics, perhaps a conservative politics that is keen to credit people with a certain right to the considerable amount of private property they have, and to leave others without such a right to any more than the lesser amount they have. A Free Will theory may also have a source in something more widely shared, a desire to give us humans a certain dignity—a standing above the rest of what exists, including what the Free Will philosophers in question would not be inclined to describe as the other animals (Kane 1996).

But the main guiding aim of a Free Will theory is likely to be a related one. In fact, it enters into the three already mentioned. It is the aim of getting to a conclusion from which it will then follow that we can be taken as absolutely responsible for our choices and our ensuing actions. It is to get to something such that it will follow that we can be taken as responsible *in a certain way*. That is all-important. As noticed in passing at the start (p. 3), there is more than one thing that can be called being held responsible for things or being credited with responsibility for things.

The aim of a Free Will theory is likely to be to make us such that we can be held responsible or credited with responsibility where our doing these latter things involves certain feelings.[2] But above all, our being responsible in this way involves our being able now to choose differently from how we do, given the present and ourselves exactly as they are and the past exactly as it was. Our choices, on this story, cannot be effects but come about somehow very differently.

Almost all historical and also most recent theories have to do with not only neural events and mental events but also something else, a self or originator. What they come to is that in each of us there exists an ongoing entity that is said to *originate* choices and decisions and hence actions, which things are not necessitated by neural events or anything else. Let us start with a very incomplete little model, later on in the adventure of Juliet and Toby.

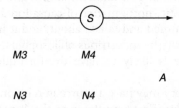

M3 is Juliet's mental event of seeing Toby on waking up one morning. M4 is her deciding a moment later to say to him that they should have a child together. This conscious event M4 will turn out to be what the model is really focused on, a free decision. The later item A is her still later action of actually saying to him that they should have a child. N3 is a neural event at the first time, and N4 a neural event at the second time, leading towards the action A. That leaves S, which is Juliet's self. It might be better to call it a Self. Certainly it is very different from the other items in the model. For a start, it is not an event, not something that occurs at a time. Rather, it is an enduring thing, moving through time from the first to the last moment shown.

The model leaves a lot out. It gives no indication of the kind of connection between the associated neural and mental bits. It gives no indication of the kind of connection between the neural bits themselves. It doesn't say anything either about the connection between the enduring thing S and, in particular, Juliet's piece of deciding, M4. The idea is that the first of these two things, her self,

---

[2] There will be more about the feelings involved in our holding people responsible and the like in chapter 8 and thereafter.

somehow gives rise to the second, the deciding. We will have to try to fill the model in.

Free Will sounds like something out of the past, as it is, but it can be brought up to date. Its supporters do this. So, as I have already implied, they do pay attention to neuroscience and neural events. They then face the question of the relation between mental and neural events, and in particular between M3 and N3 and also M4 and N4. They have two possibilities.

To speak in a loose way, they can deny necessity or nomic connection here and thereby allow for Free Will, or they can deny necessity or nomic connection at another point. Their better or least bad option, I think, is not to deny it here. This has been their common habit since they have paid attention to the brain and neuroscience, and it continues (Searle 2000; cf. Eccles and Popper).

Let us then suppose they say that each mental event is in nomic connection with the neural event at the same time. That is the one feature that this picture of the mind shares with our determinist one. But if M4 is tied in this way to N4, and the aim is to make Juliet responsible in a certain way for M4, we need to regard N4 as something other than an unavoidable effect. It can't be a real effect of N3 or anything else, or we will make its partner M4 unsatisfactorily inevitable.

This is the stage when we bring in an interpretation of physics, or rather an interpretation of the part of it that is Quantum Theory. It is in fact an interpretation of some mathematics, a way of saying what the mathematics could come to in terms of the actual world. We will be returning to the subject. What is important now is that the interpretation supposes that there are things that happen that are not effects but which are made probable by what happens before them. So we say that the neural partner N4 of the decision M4 is not an effect. It didn't have to happen. It was just something made probable by what went before, in particular the neural event N3, which went with Juliet's seeing Toby.

We now come on a first large problem. That the theory takes neural events to be made probable by antecedents is not just a case of its supporters granting something of what seems true. It is not just a necessary bow on their part in the direction of neuroscience. That is, it is not just a concession in the direction of real causal connection.

There is the reason that there has to be a pretty sure connection between N4 and subsequent neural events on the way to the action

A, or else the action *A* will be made uncertain. There will be too much chance that Juliet's words aren't at all to the effect that they should have a child, but are something else. If there is not a very high probability that items like *N4* will be followed by the right other neural events, then actions we fully and absolutely intend will on too many occasions mysteriously not happen.

So the links *after N4* have to be pretty *tight*. But then in factual consistency so do the neural links *before N4*. That is unfortunate, since the theory needs these earlier links to be pretty *loose* in order for Juliet to be held really responsible for what is tied to *N4*, her decision to speak up.

Can this large problem of seeming inconsistency really be dealt with? Maybe it can. Maybe we can tolerate the ad hoc idea that the earlier neural events are not so probable, in order to leave room for Free Will, but the later neural events are more probable, so that our behaviour doesn't involve many mysterious failures and surprises. Even so, we have not got very far in filling out the theory.

Soon after Quantum Mechanics was interpreted as the idea that there are truly unnecessitated events in the world, events not nomically connected with what precedes them, it was supposed that Free Will was thereby automatically saved. It was saved just by these random or chance events. That is, it was supposed that these events by themselves give us Free Will. But of course they don't. To put the matter briefly, I can't be any more responsible in the desired way for a mere chance event and what goes with it than for a necessitated event and what goes with it. A chance event comes out of nothing. I might be *less* responsible. In fact, until more was supposed by the hopeful philosophers, this was a case of out of the frying-pan into the fire.

The theory of Free Will we are trying to put together tries to deal with this. The neural facts, as we have seen, leave it somehow uncertain that the decision *M4* will happen. What is supposed to explain that it really does happen is Juliet's self and its activity (O'Connor 1995a; Searle 2000; Eccles and Popper; Kenny; Boyle et al.). So, in terms of the model, we need to know what *S* comes to and what its relation is to *M4*.

A couple of things are clear about *S*. If you want to explain a decision somehow, but not make it into a necessary event, it will be a good idea not to explain it by citing something that happens before it, a prior *event* that somehow gives rise to it. That will immediately raise the question of the prior event's being caused, and worse, being caused to cause the decision. An ongoing entity, a self or originator, seems better than an event.

Also, if the aim is to hold us responsible now in a way for a past choice or decision conceived as causally unconnected with our brains and characters and everything else, it is at least useful to have something definite on hand now to aim at, something that seems to be of the right sort. We need the right kind of object for our feelings. The same point applies to our having a certain moral credit.

But awful questions arise, first the question of what S comes to. What is the nature of a self? Necessarily, there is supposed to be a lot more to one of these selves than we ourselves had in mind at the beginning of chapter 3 in connection with the character of subjectivity of mental events (pp. 25–6). We speculated about an interdependent duality within mental events, involving an aspect for which another aspect exists. A self is far from being a mere aspect of mental events. It is some kind of real entity outside of them, with some kind of power with respect to them. What we can all hesitantly discern about a side of a mental event becomes something much larger. It might indeed be better to elevate it from a self to a Self.

To repeat, what is such a self supposed to be? We already have mental events and neural events on hand. What sort of thing is this originator? Is it a third sort? Does our existence involve the brain, and mental events or the flow of consciousness, and also something different from both? So it seems. Of what material is this self? We have an idea of the material of mental events or consciousness, so to speak, and an analysis of the material of neural events, but what about the self? Is it of no material at all?

If the question about its material is just out of place or wrong for some reason, what *are* we supposed to think about it? If it is *somehow* mental, in what sense is that? We need *some* information to be going on with, long before we get to such questions as whether it, unlike mental events, is not tied to but is entirely free of the brain— which, incidentally, would certainly go against what was called psychoneural intimacy.

There is a temptation into which some philosophers have fallen at this point in trying to provide it. It is the temptation to regard a self as a person within a person, a homunculus. There is a temptation to think of S as an inner person deciding M4. But this is terrible.

One familiar and smaller reason is that it seems we will then have to try to give an account of this inner Juliet along exactly the lines of the account we are now trying to give for Juliet, and so on.

Getting rhetorical or trying out deep thoughts is no help either. Nor is a deceptive kind of plain speaking. The latter happens when it is said, as if no more needed to be said, that this talk about a self is just about 'the mind' or 'a person'—in this case the real person Juliet. But plainly it's not all of the mind or all of Juliet, or even much of it, or even close to much of it, that is in question. We need something more definite. We can't just forget that the self is supposed to be able to *overcome* desires and the like which are surely elements of a person. If it chooses between inclinations, it doesn't include them.

In short, we have a second problem, still larger than the one about inconsistency in probabilities. It is a problem of clarity. All we can get hold of with respect to a self or originator is that it is in a kind of relation to decisions—we are told that it originates them. It is safe to say that no one has ever begun to answer the question of the nature of a self or originator. In fact no advocate has really faced up to the problem. All have slid by it. It seems to me likely that all future announcements of a self will be like the traditional and the recent ones (Reid; O'Connor 1995a; Clarke; Rowe).

So there are two large problems, one about inconsistency in matters of probability, and one about clarity in talk of the nature of the self. There is a third problem, related to the second, and such as to make the second worse. It is another problem of clarity. It is all very well, when asked about the relation between an originator and a decision, to say that it *originates* the decision. What does that mean? We do need to know what the connection is between S and the decision $M4$ in the model.

It is downright embarrassing to hear that the originator looks over the brain and selects neurons for activating in order to get what it wants, or rather the mental events it wants. This turns up in a large book on Free Will by a philosopher and a neurophysiologist (Eccles and Popper). It does of course involve the homunculus trouble, but that is not all. There is another much larger difficulty.

It is no good using ordinary mental verbs such as 'look over', 'select', and 'want' in order to try to describe what the relation is between an originator and a mental event. At any rate it is no good leaving the matter there. We want to know what these verbs come to in these uses, what is involved in the activities they describe. We need a general understanding of these activities. A general understanding of such activities is in fact exactly the concern of determinist and indeterminist philosophies of mind. Determinist philosophies understand such activities as a matter of standard effects. What is the opposed understanding—something in addition to the denial that the activities are such effects?

In the earlier discussion of causation in chapter 2, it was allowed that some of us ordinarily talk of our choices and decisions as being effects but would say they are not necessitated—not standard effects (pp. 16–17). And earlier we noticed various non-standard ideas of effects sometimes proposed by philosophers. There were ideas of events as just made probable by previous ones (pp. 8–10), or events vaguely owed to a vague power (p. 10), or events having previous ones as required conditions (pp. 17–18), or events having a 'usual cause' (p. 19). My own feeling is that most of us will really say, if we can be got to think about it without distractions, that our choices and decisions are best thought of in terms of standard effects. But forget about that.

In order to have a general understanding of the relation between an originator and a decision, let us try to think in terms of one or another of the non-standard ideas of causation. It doesn't matter which one. We try out the idea, as various philosophers have, that the originator by itself in some non-standard sense *causes* mental events to happen. We noticed this possibility at the beginning of the chapter about causation (pp. 8–9). To say the least, problems arise.

We need to remember, as remarked earlier, that an originator is not an event, not something that happens. In the model, S is of a different kind from everything else. There are good reasons for this from the point of view of Free Willers, as we know. If we keep events right out of it when we are thinking of an originator, as we have to, we are left with an ongoing and unchanging thing, what used to be called a substance. Putting aside our instructions, this is also what naturally comes to mind in trying to picture an originator or self.

But if the originator in the Juliet story was *the same* from start to finish, why did it somehow cause her decision M4 when it did, rather than at the earlier time of M3 or the later time of the action A? Why wasn't it *always* causing it throughout its entire career? Indeed, is there any point in saying that it 'caused' it in any sense when it occurred? Surely this causal language is so different from the standard one that it is baffling and as good as incomprehensible until more is said.

Moreover, if the originator *is* unchanging, how can it be said to cause endless numbers of *different* things, endless different decisions, as of course it is supposed to? What is the point of saying it caused Juliet to decide as she did when it might as well have resulted in her deciding the very opposite? That fact is fundamental to all non-standard causation. Remember that nothing made Juliet's decision happen, nothing necessitated it. The self didn't guarantee or ensure that decision. This last and overwhelming objection, by the way, is also one of several objections to something you may be tempted to think about, an originator that *does* change or develop over time.

One more remark here. Some of the philosophers who try to save Free Will by way of a self make use of a certain old idea taken from religion and theology. They even make use of the idea to try to define or explain the nature of a self. It is the idea of God as self-causing or cause-of-himself. What the philosophers of Free Will say about the self is that it, and certainly not an event in or of it, causes itself to make a decision—or something like that. It is hard for me to believe that time needs to be spent on trying to make sense of such stuff, wherever it turns up. Surely it does not make as much sense, even, as talk of causes as things that make other events probable, talk of causes as only required conditions, and so on.

My reason for this impatience is that causation as we know it, whatever it is, and all ideas of causation other than this one of self-causation, involve a relation between two things, a dyadic relation between two non-identical things. That is what you can call an axiom about causation. So if someone talks of exactly C causing exactly C, they are not talking at all of the sort of thing we know something about. They need to start explaining from the beginning, rather than assume they can start with a certain understanding on our part.

Can this bundle of problems be dealt with by making a certain move? Can we help out advocates of Free Will by offering them the use of our clearer ideas of causation? Of standard or ordinary causation?

In fact, have at least some of us not implicitly been thinking of the originator as something like a causal circumstance? Certainly this is natural. It avoids some difficulties, since it is satisfactorily impossible to think that a whole causal circumstance persists through time but has its effect only at one moment rather than another. It is also satisfactorily impossible to think that a causal circumstance can give rise to a multitude of different things, and at one moment to opposite things. But, despite the advantages, we simply *cannot* take the originator as a causal circumstance. It doesn't guarantee anything. Is there another possibility? What if we think of an originator as just a *cause*, just a part of a causal circumstance (see p. 12)?

We now have an idea of Free Will, very different indeed from the model we have been considering. The originator becomes one constant or ongoing element of various causal circumstances for decisions. The other items in each particular circumstance might be different mental events, including desires, inclinations, and so on. We certainly face a difficulty. If such a causal circumstance really is a causal circumstance, then one particular decision and no other has to be the upshot. If it is to serve the ends of a Free Will theory, we are going to have to make the new story very different, and very mysterious.

It will have to be that when everything else is in place for a decision, it is up to the originator whether or not to pull its weight. Certainly an originator has traditionally been thought to be able to defeat desires, go against the person's whole nature, rise over the past, choose the path of duty, and so on. But then we seem to be back with the originator as decisive by itself, again something like a causal circumstance—which in fact it can't be. We get pretty much the same bafflements as before. How could what is unchanging give rise to something *or* its opposite? What *is* this obscure activity?

We do not get out of these various difficulties about the relation between an originator and decisions by turning to seemingly different conceptions of an originator, perhaps as a faculty of the mind called the Will, or an active power, or the Self-Conscious Mind. It is not clear what these entities are, but it does seem that the different ways of talking simply inherit the various difficulties. The Will, for example, is sometimes said to be a rational disposition (Kenny 1975). Such a thing has the power to produce something all by itself, but it may not. But then what are we to understand about its working when it does work? Why does it work at one time rather than another? How can it give rise to a different and opposite decision from the one it does give rise to? All this seems to be the same mystery again.

One summary of the mystery is that we are given no explanation of why or how decisions and the like are supposed to come about, and thus given no content to talk of their being in our control, or their being such that we are responsible for them. The sad fact is that these theories seem to fall back into being what we noticed earlier, and what they must of course try to add to, the idea owed to Quantum Theory that decisions and choices are a matter of mere chance events. This falling-back does indeed wreck responsibility and dignity and special rights and so on.

In my opinion the least embarrassing response to the request for an explanation of the relation between an originator and decisions is that an explanation cannot be given. We have to regard this relation as primitive or unanalysable. The situation is to be taken as like one with a language or a logical system. Not every term can be broken down into others—there has to be at least one term that is taken as clear without being explained in terms of others. We start with that and explain other things in terms of it.

What this response comes to is that there exists a relation between an originator and a decision such that the person in question can in a way be held responsible for the decision. More can be said about what it is to hold a person responsible, but nothing can be said about the relation itself. We just somehow understand it. This may seem suspicious, or a cop-out, and of course it does not help with the two earlier problems, about inconsistency in connection with probability and the very nature of an originator. But it is a possible position. Something like it is held by a very acute philosopher who has been to the fore among Incompatibilists. Freedom is incompatible with determinism, he said, but this freedom remains a mystery (van Inwagen 2002).

After all this, it may come as no surprise, despite the temptations of the idea of an originator, that there are philosophers of Free Will who have given up entirely on the idea. They argue for origination without an originator or self. They have no truck with a non-event or unchanging substance somehow giving rise to choices and decisions. They have nothing to say about self-causation. They take S right out of our model (p. 42) and try to make satisfactory sense of the decision in other ways. The general idea is that you can explain Free Will and save the desired kind of responsibility just by

seeing that items like *M3*, *N3*, *M4*, *N4*, and *A* stand in certain relations. By such means you can explain why or how decisions come
about and are in our control and why we are in a way responsible
for them.

Of the various relations mentioned, perhaps the simplest is that a
choice or decision, although it is not a standard effect, is owed to a
reason. This reason may be identified somehow with a belief, a
desire, a combination of those two, an intention, or something of
the sort. To go back to the little model, but with *S* taken out of it,
what explains *M4*, Juliet's deciding to say to Tony that they should
have a child, is her reason, *M3*—something like the look of him that
happy morning. Indeterminism was true of the whole episode. It
may be added, bravely, that *M4* was not an effect in any sense at all,
however special. *M4* is explained just by the reason for it (cf. Ginet;
Nozick; Searle 2000).

This certainly seems to fail. Speaking very generally, we have two
ideas of reasons, the first being of what it is natural to call *good
reasons*. Such a reason is a proposition that makes another proposition true. Take a first proposition that itself has two parts: *if* I am
an uncle then someone is my nephew or niece, and I *am* an uncle.
That is a conclusive reason for a second proposition: I *do* have a
nephew or niece. Of course the first proposition does not *cause* the
second—because, for a start, neither proposition is an event, something that happens. Also, the relation between the reason and the
conclusion, as we say, is just a logical one.

Our second idea of a reason is of a belief or desire or whatever, a
conscious event, that causes another such event, say another belief
or a choice or decision. Such a reason may have as its content a
reason in the first sense—a good reason. But the later event does
not occur because of that logical relation, but rather because it is
the effect of the earlier event. One proof is that the logical relation
could exist, and the person in fact think of the good reason, without the second event's happening at all. We aren't always logical.

What follows from this is that if you try to explain an event by
citing a reason, you are already in the business of giving a causal
explanation of some sort. If you deny that you are in this business,
you need to begin to try to tell a whole new story. You can't depend
on reasons where they are no more than terms of logical relations.
You need an explanation of *events*.

There are other attempts to make a relation of origination clear.

Some use the ideas noticed in connection with an originator. A decision is said to be self-causing. Or it is said to be an effect only in the sense that it was preceded by something that made it probable, or was a required condition for it, or had an uncertain power to produce it, or was something like a 'usual cause'. If we no longer face the awful problems having to do with an unchanging originator sailing through time, we do have other problems with these ideas.

The main one is that these various items simply seem to fail to give us an explanation of the choice or decision. We get no reason to think that the choice or decision is in the control of the person. The simple fact is that we are to understand that the earlier event could have occurred entirely without the so-called effect. That must be true because all that is said is consistent with the assumed indeterminism—there being no causal circumstance for the so-called effect, no necessitation of it.

This is not necessarily the slightly controversial claim that all explanations of events are standard causal explanations. Rather, it can be the proposition that if you give up standard causation, you really do need to supply some other general idea of explanation. You can't leave a hole where there was something before. And you can't fill the hole by giving it the name of being some sort of funny cause. Funny causes, by definition, don't say why things actually happen.

As it seems to me, this is the situation of the philosopher (Kane 2002b) who has laboured most manfully to explain origination without recourse to an originator. To talk of choices and decisions as effects in the sense of being probable, he adds a good deal. Choices and decisions are the results of efforts, the outcomes of struggles, the upshots of willings, the resolving of conflicts between duty and desire. They are, perhaps most importantly, self-forming actions.

All this is conveyed to us as if these descriptions themselves are supposed to give us an explanation of the coming-about of the decisions. But if the various verbs and locutions are deprived of a standard causal content, which they must be, and given only some content having to do with probabilities, the choices and decisions remain unexplained. For all that has been said, any one of them might never have happened.

That is not all that can be said at this point, particularly about the matter of probability and effects. Probability is a difficult and disputed subject, as was remarked earlier, even if it is clear that an event's having been made probable by something is not the same as the thing's having been a causal circumstance for it. But this is consistent with another clear and good idea—the possibility that our talk of the probability of an event's happening actually *presupposes and depends on* there really being a standard causal explanation of the event. This bad news for Free Will philosophy is roughly as follows.

What is it for an earlier event A to have made it 95 per cent probable that a later event B would occur? A good idea about this has to do with the fact, of which you have already heard, that typically we don't know exactly and fully what is in a causal circumstance for B. And that typically we have a pretty good idea. We know in what situation a causal circumstance tends to occur.

Suppose it has been our experience that in 95 per cent of the situations in which event A occurred, it was followed by B. We say B is 95 per cent probable with respect to A, and what this means is just that in 95 per cent of the situations in which A occurs, there is precisely a causal circumstance for B. That leaves B as just probable with respect to A, and not the effect of A as a causal circumstance. But the fact of probability simply presupposes that B is the standard effect of something. As I say, bad news if you want to put probability together with indeterminism.

Let us notice just one other attempt to make sense of origination. Some advocates of Free Will, including the philosopher lately mentioned, have said that decisions are explained *teleologically*—that is, in terms of their goal. They are explained by what they lead to. This ancient line of thought is owed to the fact that we can indeed say things like this: *Birds have hollow bones because that enables them to fly better* and *We perspire because that reduces our bodily temperature.* But this talk, as almost everyone agrees, cannot really give us the conclusion that effects by themselves explain their causes. That seems to be an astonishing idea.

Attempts have been made to make teleology less astonishing (G. A. Cohen). They have not succeeded, and nothing is going to get us to agree that the occurrence of a decision is explained just by what it results in. In connection with the birds and our perspiration, what will come to mind is an evolutionary story, which really is standardly causal. To say birds have hollow bones because that

enables them to fly better is to say there is an evolutionary explanation of the hollow bones—some types of creature have survived
because of the advantage to their predecessors of their hollow
bones. If we turn the Free Will theory's teleological explanation
into some standard causal one, however, we will defeat its main
purpose (Honderich 1982).

Last but not least, it is likely that a Free Will theory really cannot
get rid of the embarrassment of an originator. It has to have *something* that is going to be responsible. A past decision itself, whether
it was probable or self-causing or teleological or anything else, isn't
what we hold responsible for actions or give a kind of moral credit
to for actions. If a philosopher says it is not a person in an ordinary
sense who is responsible, something of certain traits, desires and so
on, he will indeed need to offer us something more than a choice or
decision in certain relations. We don't put past decisions in jail
either.

Have I been too hard on the philosophy of Free Will, too judgemental? Well, have a look for yourself at efforts to set out clear,
consistent and complete accounts (Kane 2002a; O'Connor 1995b).
As for our project of setting out a determinist philosophy, we need
to finish it by looking at the relation of conscious events to subsequent actions. We will then come to a final judgement about the
clarity, consistency, and completeness of the two philosophies, and
then really look at the question which has already been pushing in,
their truth.

5

OUR ACTIONS

WHEN we act, our bodies or parts of them move. In the case of arms and legs, it seems simple. In the case of typing on a keyboard not so simple, and in the case of signing contracts and carrying on a conversation not simple at all. Still, to take the last example, saying good morning to someone does involve throat and lip movements. Shall we say that, fundamentally, actions just are movements or sequences of movements? As usual, 'fundamentally' is a bit vague, but there are good reasons for resisting the idea that actions come down to movements.

Here is one. If a snowball looks like hitting me, I duck. Certain movements of my body happen. But if by some extraordinary chance the very same movements had happened as a result of a friend's pushing my head down, my movements would not be an action. Nor would the very same movements be an action if I did not see the snowball and they came about by accident. The movements wouldn't be an action either if the futuristic philosopher's friend was on hand—he is the imaginable neuroscientist who sends impulses directly to my muscles to produce exactly the right movements at the right time.

What this suggests is that my actions somehow involve my mental or conscious events. My movements when my friend pushed me were not an action of mine because they had nothing to do with what was in my mind. So with the accidental movements and the movements produced by direct muscle stimulation. There have been philosophers suspicious of mental events who have hoped to give an account of actions without bringing them in. Some have tried to dispense with mental events by saying actions are movements that hang together in something like what Wittgenstein called a form of life, but it is hard to share their hopes that the account works (Kenny 1975).

Shall we then say that an action is something that has a bodily and a mental part? That an action consists in a movement together with such a mental event as an intention? (Or a stillness together with a mental event, since standing to attention seems to be an action?) Several philosophers have thought so, but perhaps they should have thought again (McGinn; cf. O'Shaughnessy). There are two reasons for thinking that an action is not a compound made up of a mental part and another part.

The first is that we see an action. As it seems, we see all of an action, or we can. If part of an action was a mental event, we could not ever see or otherwise perceive all of an action. Each time someone raised a glass, we could not be seeing all of it, but rather seeing part of it and inferring or guessing about another part. That does not sound right. If I am asked in court about the murder done in front of me, I am not being asked if I saw part of it and inferred the rest.

The second reason that an action is not a compound of an intention and a movement has to do with the fact that typically the intention or part of the intention precedes the movement in time. But if the intention is actually part of the action, then we have to accept something that we really cannot. A nod is an action. If the nod included a prior intention, then a nod begins before the head moves. A speech always starts before you can hear it. There is something wrong with that.

It seems clear that we have to get a mental event into the story, and that it cannot be part of an action. There is a clear way of doing this. The aim is to distinguish the class of actions from the class of mere movements by reference to a mental event. In fact we can distinguish things by way of items that are not parts of them. We can distinguish a certain refrigerator from what we may call identical ones by the fact that it is the only one that is yours. That is a bit complicated, but there are simpler cases. We commonly distinguish things by their causes. These candlesticks are the ones made in Michigan, those are the ones made in Derbyshire. We also distinguish things by their effects. Simpler still, we distinguish things by where they are, their location. Their locations aren't a part of them.

In short, we can take actions to be those movements that are in some relation to certain sorts of mental events of the person in question. A decent account of actions will then have three parts. It will identify the mental event or mental events more precisely. That is not entirely easy. It will say what the relation to a movement is. Thirdly, it will deal with some problems about movements. If I hit you with a snowball, is the action only where the movement is?

We do need a decent account of actions in order to have a complete theory of determinism. We need the part that I referred to earlier as Action Determinism (p. 31). This, as we know, has to do with how actions come about. If this part is less important than the first two, it is none the less essential. Also, there have been philosophers who have supposed that determinism collapses over the matter of actions.

Some have said that determinism is an impossible theory because it has the logical consequence that there aren't any actions. We never act. It would certainly be in trouble if that were true. The main line of thought here is simple (Chisholm 1976). It is that an action is necessarily a movement that is related to a self or originator—to help the argument along, the self or originator is often referred to as the person—and there aren't any of those if determinism is true. There isn't origination. So there can't be any actions.

We have already spent rather a lot of time with this kind of self, and need not return to it. What we need to do in order to deal with this sort of objection to determinism is to try to show that a decent account of actions can be given without recourse to an originating self. It is possible to have some doubt in advance about the idea of actions as tied to originators, by the way. It seems reasonable to assume we have a pretty clear idea of actions. Could that be the case if the idea included a self of the obscure kind?

What typically precedes what we call an action is an intention. More precisely, what typically precedes an action is an intention that comes well before it in time, maybe the day before or earlier. Let us start with intentions of this kind, which are not actually issuing in an action. They can be called *inactive or forward-looking intentions*. What is such a thing?

It must involve a desire or want. I cannot intend to go to the consciousness conference in Tucson by plane tomorrow if there is no sense in which I now want to do so. It may be, of course, that there is a sense in which I don't want to take the trip. Indeed, the prospect may be disagreeable. The flight may take eleven hours. But if I really do intend to go, I must somehow want to. In this connection some philosophers have tried to distinguish what they call volitive from appetitive desires. Distinguishing them isn't easy, but volitive desires are related to determination to do something, and appetitive desires have to do with pleasure (W. A. Davis 1983b). An action always involves a volitive desire.

I must also have some idea of how to try to do the thing in question, say get to the airport. I cannot intend to do a thing if I really have no idea at all about how to do it—or about how to find out how to do it. Of course there are situations where what I have is only the most uncertain idea that something might work. But I do need some minimum of what can be called instrumental or means-end belief (cf. Bratman; Mele).

There is also another kind of belief I must have, also a little difficult to specify. I need a predictive belief. I can't now intend to do what I am certain I won't do. If I absolutely believe now that I won't get on the plane to Tucson, I don't intend to do so. I may intend to try, where that is some different action, but I don't intend to get on the plane to Tucson. That is not to say that to intend to do something I have to be certain that I will do it. I have to believe that it is probable. How probable? Let us slide by that question.

It is sometimes supposed that this is enough for an intention: a desire, an instrumental belief, and a predictive belief. It is sometimes supposed the first two are enough. That may not be right. Suppose I now want or desire to go to an auction tomorrow and make a bid for a picture. I also know how, and I think I will. But that is not my whole state of mind. I also think something strange indeed. It is that I will fall into a kind of absent-mindedness and will make a bid in an extraordinary way. I think the bid will really have nothing to do with my now wanting to buy the picture or my two beliefs now. It seems that if this is my state of mind now, I don't now intend to bid for the picture.

What we have to add to our analysis in order to deal with this is the idea that my present desire and beliefs will be the explanation of my movement tomorrow. My movement tomorrow will be dependent on them. We can label this fact about my intention a *dependency-belief*.

There seems to be one last closely related thing. To see it, we again need some imagining. Suppose my state of mind today is as so far described, but has one more thing to it. I believe that the bid will come about because my desire and my three beliefs terrify me into it. The story will be that my hand goes up because I am in a state of shock over my desire to part with so much money and what I am contemplating doing. If I believe all that today, do I intend to make a bid tomorrow? That is doubtful. Let us then add that I have to believe today that what will happen tomorrow is that my desire and so on will motivate me to act in the ordinary and familiar way (Davidson 1980).

So much for an inactive or forward-looking intention. One of these consists in a desire and the four discriminable beliefs. (It should be no surprise that an intention is this kind of complex or combination. Ordinary emotions are also of this kind. For a start, they include both thinking and feeling.) An action seems at least typically to involve another kind of intention. It occurs immediately before or at the start of a movement and also during it. There are two things different about what we can call an *active intention*, which is also what used to be called a volition or an act of willing.

The first thing is that it is almost certain to involve different beliefs. When I am actually sitting in the auction room, behind the very large man, I believe that I will have to bid by means of sticking my hand up very high, and that I will stick my hand up very high. I had neither of these anticipations yesterday, nor any associated dependency-belief or motivation-belief.

The second difference between active and inactive intentions is not at all easy to describe. It is the kind of thing that you can want to avoid out of a determination to be clear at any cost. But it cannot be avoided. When I actually act, I do something that can be called giving a command to a part of my body. That is to speak loosely and metaphorically, of course. But better a metaphor than nothing. What can also be said, although the words can be used for other purposes, is that I am executive, or try to do the thing in question, or set myself to do it. There is no counterpart to this fact with an inactive intention.

Active intentions or volitions have not always been popular ideas in the philosophy of mind and psychology. The doctrine of behaviourism in its several forms, for example, was an enemy of mental events and in particular of active intentions. Behaviourism is over, and its true successors will not thrive long. There is good reason for that in connection with active intentions, since it is hard to deny that active intentions as we know them do exist or occur.

One reason for accepting them is that on the present account they are not nearly so elusive as they have sometimes been supposed to be. They are in good part like inactive intentions although they have an additional distinctive part, the executive part. One other reason for accepting them is that someone who is suffering paralysis, but does not yet know about it, may have the fullest confidence that he has clenched the fist behind his back. Presumably that is because of the event of his actively intending to do so. What is also worth noting is that opposition to active intentions has to do with the fact that they can only be recollected, not focused on while they are occurring. But the same is true of my half-noticing something in my environment a moment ago, and that certainly happened.

What has been said so far has been in a way guarded. It is that actions are *typically* preceded by inactive intentions and *at least typically* preceded and accompanied by active intentions. Is it the case that for a movement to count as an action, it *must* be preceded or accompanied by either? Does the concept of an action necessarily include either?

It seems we can get the short answer to that by thinking about certain simple cases. People on television for the first time are inclined to fidget, to make little movements. It is hard to deny that the movements are actions. It seems impossible to say that an idle movement I make now, say touching my ear or the flower on the desk, of which I am fully conscious, is not an action. But in none of these cases was there an inactive intention.

We can conclude that actions are not partly to be defined as movements that are preceded by inactive or forward-looking intentions. They often are so preceded, but that is not necessary. We can also conclude that actions *are* partly to be defined as movements preceded and accompanied by active intentions. If one of my movements involves no such thing, it is no more an action than the reflex movement of my foot when the doctor taps my knee.

So much for the first part of an account of actions. The second part is the relation between the active intention and the movement. It can be dealt with quickly. Part of what is involved has been implicit in what has been said of intentions, and the other part will have come to mind.

If intentions involve beliefs about the coming movements, and in particular a predictive belief that a particular movement will happen, then it seems intentions somehow *represent* movements. They seem in some way to describe or picture or refer to them. In the case of very simple movements of no consequence in themselves, what may be true is that we have a kind of tactile image of what is going to happen.

If I have an intention, and what happens the next moment bears no resemblance to it, is not represented by it at all, it seems that I did not act. One thing that will help to persuade us of this is that actions are things for which people are held responsible. If I have a full-blooded intention, however else it is connected to the movement that follows, I am surely not responsible for the movement if it was in no way what I had in mind. I may be blamed or praised for the intention but not for the movement. There are borderline cases of course. What are we to say of the man who fully and really intended to kiss his bride at the altar, and shakes hands instead?

If intentions represent movements when the movements are actions, we also take them to be in a second relation to them. They are causes of them. There seems no doubt about this part of our conception of an action (Davidson 1980; A. I. Goldman). Indeed this is the one part of a theory of determinism that is a matter of ordinary belief. The causal connection is as essential as the representative connection. Suppose I have a full-blooded intention, and the movement that follows is on exactly the right lines, represented by the intention. Still, if the movement were a matter of real chance, or were caused by someone interfering with my muscles in a way that had nothing to do with my intention, then the movement wasn't an action of mine.

We have had a look at the mental events that precede the movements that are actions, and the relation between the mental events and the actions. Finally, just a word about the movements themselves. It is possible to be a little puzzled here, but perhaps not for long. One question is the one mentioned earlier. If I hit you with a snowball, is my action only where my movement is? 'Hitting somebody with a snowball' can be thought to describe more than an action. If we confine ourselves just to the question of where the action was, there seems no real obstacle to saying it was exactly where the movement was. We will say something different about something else, the action's effects, but that does not matter. So there is no difficulty in the way of saying that actions *are* movements that have certain antecedents (cf. Hornsby 1998).

When does an action take place? If I shoot my neighbour today and he dies tomorrow, when do I kill him? If the killing partly takes place tomorrow, then the killing can't be my relevant movements today. On reflection, there is no need at all to fall into doubt. I shoot him today and what happens tomorrow is an effect of that. As a result of that effect, it may become true to say that I killed him, that my shooting was also a killing. But that does not make my action happen tomorrow.

We now have a definition of an action adequate to our needs, and so are in a position to state an Action Determinism, the third and final part of a full theory of determinism. There is one slightly embarrassing problem. The definition we have got of an action comes to something like this: *a bodily movement caused and of course represented by an active intention.* The problem is that what we want to say, as the third part of the full theory, is that *actions are caused by mental and neural events, say as they are conceived in the Union Theory* (see p. 30), *and the mental events include a relevant active intention.* But if we understand actions in the way defined, that is a pretty point-less statement, not worth making. What it states, to put it one way, is that what are caused by intentions are caused by intentions. It is an analytic or necessarily true statement, like *All bachelors are unmarried.*

What this reflects is what was mentioned a moment ago, that this third part of our determinism is believed by everybody except one or two really characterful philosophers of Free Will (Anscombe 1963). As a result, it has got into language, specifically our under-standing of the word 'action'. If that is reassuring, it also poses us a little problem. We are rightly convinced that even if the answer is straightforward, there is a real question to which Action Determin-ism gives an answer. That is, there is something other than the pointless question of whether what is caused by an intention is caused by an intention. Also, we do need such a question. In con-sidering the overall question of the truth of determinism, we do not want part of it settled by definition or language.

The solution to the problem, which does depend on our having clarified our conception of an action, is to turn to a related concep-tion. We can turn to what is a less specific definition. We define an action in a general way as a movement *somehow owed to* and represented by an active intention. When we now ask if actions are *caused* by active intentions, we have a real question.

That completes a theory of determinism, or at least a sketch of a theory. What it comes to is something like this:

(1) Each mental or conscious event, including each choosing or deciding, is in nomic connection with an associated neural event. The neural event by itself or together with some other non-mental thing necessitated the mental one. That is, since the non-mental things happened, whatever else had been happening, the mental event would still have happened just as it did. That is Mind–Brain Determinism.

(2) The mental event and the neural event, to think in particular of the Union Theory, were the effect of a causal sequence, whose initial causal circumstance had in it early neural and bodily events and also certain environmental events—no mental events. That is Initiation Determinism.

(3) Each action, in a general sense of the word, is the effect of a causal sequence whose initial circumstance included the right active intention. Action Determinism.

The three parts hook together. In them do we have something that is clear, consistent, and worked-out? Do we have a respectable philosophy of mind and action? We could go further, but in my opinion we have got such a thing, or anyway a good sketch. We can do with a model of the thole thing, again understood in terms of the Union Theory, one particular Mind–Body Determinism.

$M3$ and $N3$ are one psychoneural pair. This pair together with the later environmental event $E2$ makes a causal circumstance for the pair made up of $M4$ and $N4$. $M4$ is an active intention or part of one. The pair it is in, together with some bodily event $B1$, makes a causal circumstance for the action A.

With hindsight, now that we have a theory of determinism in front of us, what is to be said of the philosophy of mind and action in terms of origination or Free Will? Certainly you have not been in the company of the most sympathetic of expositors of this alternative. Still, I did try. In my opinion this philosophy is less clear, less consistent, and less worked-out. I am not its harshest critic, incidentally. Others (G. Strawson) say worse, as we shall see (p. 102). It does seem to me sufficiently intellectually respectable to deserve consideration. In one way, as we shall eventually see (chapter 8), it is very important and deserves exactly as much consideration as determinism.

By way of a sketch, it comes to something like this:

Choices and decisions, at least some of them, are different from other mental events in that they are originated by the self or originated in another way having to do with their relations to preceding reasons and the like. That is to say that they are owed to the self or come about in such a way, of which no more can be said, that the person is in a way responsible for them. In any case, he or she could have decided otherwise given things exactly as they were and the past exactly as it was.

Which of these two pictures is true? That is the next business.

6

NEUROSCIENCE AND QUANTUM THEORY

I F this were a better world, in which you had more time and diligence than most of us have in this one, you might be reading something better than this chapter. I have in mind a large textbook surveying neuroscience—the family of overlapping subjects including neurophysiology, neuroanatomy, neurobiology, neurochemistry, neuropsychology, and so on (Kandel et al.; Kuffler et al.; Carlson; Cotman and McGaugh). Reading the textbook would be better for the reason that it would persuade you that neuroscience is in a way not inconclusive or speculative. It is not inconclusive or speculative in a way that philosophically-minded people are likely to suppose, and some dearly want to suppose. Of course neuroscience does contain very many unsettled matters and hypotheses, to say nothing of disagreement and great ignorance. But in my view it also contains more than enough clear hard facts to enable us to choose between the two philosophies of mind.

Since you are substituting this chapter for the textbooks, the first thing to consider is neurons, about which a word was said earlier (p. 26). Our mental lives are bound up with these most important elements of our brains and central nervous systems. Each of them is a cell into which go roots or dendrites, usually short, not unlike the roots of plants and trees. Out of each neuron goes a trunk or axon, usually long. The roots are for input to the main body of the cell, and the trunk for output. At the end of the trunk is a synapse or connection with other items, usually roots of other neurons.

The input and output are electrochemical in nature. To begin with input to a root, chemical substances called neurotransmitters are released or secreted across a synapse, and thus contribute to whether the neuron goes active or not. Some chemical inputs promote activity and some inhibit it. The activity is electrical and well understood. It consists in the passage of electrical impulses down the trunk of the neuron. These impulses occur in patterns, and result at the end of the trunk in the release of neurotransmitters across synapses to other neurons.

A general truth about all these building blocks of the brain and nervous system is that their operation is indubitably taken to be causal. It is taken to be causal by just about all working neuroscientists. No question can arise about that. Certainly what happens in neurons is partly spoken of by way of ordinary verbs like 'release', 'contribute to', 'occur', and 'issue in'. And certainly the general verb 'to cause' is not common in neuroscience. These facts are sometimes remarked on, but neither of them raises any doubt that the operation of neurons is taken without hesitation to be causal.

If there were a doubt, there would be the same doubt about meteorology, engineering, and motor mechanics. In and outside of science we commonly use many kinds of what in fact are causal verbs, starting with 'push' and 'pull', rather than the verb 'to cause'. This is because of their greater informativeness or easiness. There is no difficulty in giving for each of these verbs an analysis that uses the word 'cause' and the like. It is also to be noticed that in neuroscience like the rest of science, the nouns are commonly causal. That is, things are defined in terms of their causal properties. This is true of 'neuron' itself, as indicated by our quick definition above.

The unanimity or near-unanimity among working neuroscientists, not unsettled by a physicist or two seeking to import an interpretation of their Quantum Theory into neuroscience (Penrose), provides clear and strong evidence for our theory of determinism. To speak differently, such support is provided by the general fact that neurons are causal. More particularly, this first general fact provides support for Initiation Determinism, about the causal history of mental and neural events, which is fundamental to the whole theory.

Do you say that a brain and central nervous system has in it a stunningly large number of neurons? That a single thought may be involved with millions of neurons? And that for this reason alone neuroscience is in good or large part concerned with relations between groups, systems, and types of neurons? That is true. But can it give you the idea that causation only works at the bottom level of the brain? Well, it would be an odd house or machine whose elements were all causal but whose large substructures were not.

We will come to that matter of higher levels in a minute, but first let us go back to the first part of the theory of determinism— Mind–Brain Determinism—and notice a second general fact of neuroscience. We took up Mind–Brain Determinism for roughly the double reason that we supposed mental events are intimately connected with neural events and that theories that actually identify them are not acceptable. In connection with the supposition of psychoneural intimacy, neuroscience also offers us a general supporting truth, a general fact.

Neuroscience puts our mental events into categories, not very different from our ordinary categories—thinking, the experience of seeing, desiring, intending, and so on. It associates these categories with particular parts of the brain—regions, lobes, and areas. The parts of the limbic system have to do with emotion, motivation, and goal-directedness, among other things (Greenfield 2000). There are particular parts of the cerebral cortex related to sensation and perception, and areas that enter into the planning, beginning, and control of movement. Various areas, say Broca's speech area, have to do with the higher functions—reasoning and the like.

This is the fact of what is called localization—categories of mental events or functions being assigned to particular localities in the brain. The simple brain charts of the notorious Gall of the early nineteenth century, who also went in for phrenology, have long been discarded. So too has the work of the 'narrow localizationists' later on. It is now commonly said that no part of the brain works alone. None of this takes away from the general fact of localization. It does not by itself provide evidence for psychoneural intimacy quite as strong as the generalization about all neurons being causal does for the proposition about the causation of mental and neural events. But certainly it must make us lean in the direction of psychoneural intimacy.

Let us pass by what can be said about a general neuroscientific fact or two that support Action Determinism, about our actions being certain effects. The situation is much the same as with Initiation Determinism, only yet better for the determinist. Instead, let us turn from general to more particular facts, although about groups, systems, and types of neurons. Let us first glance at some of these that bear on the matter of mind and brain, the intimate connection between mental and neural events, and thus on our Mind–Brain Determinism. These can only be bits and pieces of evidence whose reporting actually does a kind of injustice to the state of knowledge within neuroscience.

There has been a great deal of research into memory and learning, which is to say mental activities dependent on previous experience. It is true that the subject of the investigations is usually taken to be connections between neural facts and what is spoken of as behaviour. The behaviour, however, is plainly taken as evidence of mentality, and would not attract attention if this were not true. Neuroscience, as may come as a surprise, is not generally behaviourist in the only senses that matter. In fact it is far from actually denying the existence of mental events or consciousness, and it is about as far from being unconcerned with them.

Some of the most dramatic research into memory in the past involved the electrical stimulation of particular bits of the cortex of patients by means of inserted electrodes. The stimulation was accompanied by 'flashbacks' reported by the patients. Repeated stimulations of the same bits were accompanied by identical recall-experiences. Contemporary research involving electronic scanning and much else has moved far beyond these findings, but in the same direction. There are related stories to be told in connection with the emotions. So with pain and pleasure.

With respect to consciousness itself, which is to say mental events generally, there is again a dramatic body of research. It has to do with the left and right cerebral hemispheres of the brain and the large tract of neurons that connects them, the corpus callosum. When this tract is severed by surgical operation, as in the treatment of severe epilepsy, the result is not only a 'split-brain' but in a clear sense two minds. The patient no longer has what is often called the unity of consciousness. There is the conclusion to be drawn that in an ordinary person, unity of consciousness is in intimate connection with a certain neural structure.

So with conceptualization, thought, problem-solving, reasoning, imagination, and the like. It used to be traditional in surveys of neuroscience to come to these higher functions last and to say that little or nothing is known about them in terms of the brain. That kind of rhetoric was understandable, but it is consistent with something else. We are not at all without facts in this neighbour-hood. These have much to do with what is fundamental to the higher functions—language and speech. It is very far from true that nothing is known of what are sometimes called the neural sub-strates of language and speech. By way of just one detail, there is extensive knowledge of the neural accompaniments of various dis-orders, some of them clearly intellectual, and therefore of the dif-ferent neural accompaniments of ordinary orderly thought.

The upshot of all this can be put simply. Neuroscience proves psychoneural intimacy. That is, mental events have what we can call neural intimates, and the other way on. Mental events somehow go together necessarily with their associated neural events, and the other way on. According to our previous line of argument, this must issue either in our actually identifying mental with neural events or else in our taking them to be in some kind of nomic or 'whatever-else' connection—and the first option, a true Identity Theory, is not a serious starter.

Further, if the proof of intimacy supports Mind–Brain Deter-minism in this way, it also does something else as important for us. It rules out what is fundamental to the Free Will theory, which is its free-floating self or originator. Whatever else was supposed to be true of a self or originator, it was supposed to be above and beyond the brain.

We could turn now to more particular rather than general neu-roscientific evidence for our proposition about Initiation Determin-ism. We might at this point go through some of the categories of our mental events again, one category having to do with learning and memory, another with conceptualization, thought, and the like, and so on. We would come upon a lot of particular facts, a lot of verifying detail. We might give attention to what is entirely relevant, research on the lower animals. For instance, the genetic research that has involved the breeding of 'maze-bright' and 'maze-dull' rats. Let us turn instead to another kind of reflection on neuroscience and Initiation Determinism.

Does neuroscience support a story about neural events as causal or a story about neural events *and* their associated mental events as causal? Our Initiation Determinism involves the second kind of story. Does what was reported about the causal functioning of the neuron, and what might be reported about larger causal linkages, really support our chosen idea that what does the causing is pairs of mental and neural events as distinct from just neural events? We have supposed so, but it is possible to think the contrary, that neuroscience says that it is neural events that do the causing.

To my mind neuroscience can be said to support both stories, in different ways. But to take something else first, it certainly does not *deny* our own proposition. It does not deny that the causal circumstance for a later mental event or an action included a mental event. There are various points here.

One is that it *does* deny a related thing which needs to be distinguished. It is against the idea that a neural event tied to a mental event might be the upshot of a process that was at some moments or in some segments not at all neural or otherwise bodily. That idea of bodily gaps is what seems to sink the Interactionism noticed in Chapter 4. But there is a real difference between saying neural events come from processes that are always neural or otherwise bodily, and saying that neural events come from processes that are always neural or otherwise bodily and also never mental. Only the latter thing conflicts with our view.

A second point about a mental event's causal circumstance itself including a mental event is that neuroscience is not much concerned to find whole causal circumstances for events. In this it is like most of science. What it contents itself with, typically, is causes or other parts of causal circumstances. This is in accord with something often mentioned. Despite illusions to the contrary, much of science is not much concerned to establish laws. Neuroscience chooses not to concern itself with the mental parts of certain causal circumstances. The reason in brief is that they have not been thought to be so open to scientific investigation as the neural parts.

A third point. To deny that mental events play a part in explaining actions and other mental events would be to go back to epiphenomenalism, the nineteenth-century doctrine noticed in chapter 3. But the proposition that the mental events of my desires, beliefs, and so on *are* part of the explanation of my actions is accepted by almost everyone. Epiphenomenalism is not really asserted in neuroscience, despite the fact that neuroscience contains some rare moments of shaky philosophizing.

A last point has to do with the wider question of whether neuroscience might be committed only to causes and not to causal circumstances, whatever might be in the circumstances. Can it be thought to support Free Will by denying causal circumstances?

That is out of the question. It plainly makes use of the standard conception of causation. As was implicit in our opening reflections on causation, that conception includes causal circumstances. To assert a cause of something in the standard way *is* to be committed to a causal circumstance. This is so for the reason among others that causes have effects, and effects are by standard understanding owed to causal circumstances.

So—if neuroscience does not actually deny causation by both a neural event and the associated mental event, does it support it? It supports the neural part explicitly and the mental part implicitly. That it supports mental causation in an implicit rather than an explicit way is quite sufficient reassurance. It enables us to conclude again that neuroscience gives at least clear and strong support to our theory of determinism.

You may say that that is all very well, but there is also another large fact. That is the large fact of Quantum Theory, a major part of the physics of the twentieth century and since then. This large fact goes the other way, you say. And, you add, it is somehow more important than neuroscience. Its evidence outweighs the evidence of neuroscience. Physicists make up a kind of priesthood of science, and they need to be listened to last.

What has commonly been said of Quantum Theory, although no longer so confidently, is that it shows that at the level of very small particles, well below the level of neurons, determinism is not a fact. At this micro-level, whatever may be true above it at the macro-level, things happen that are chance and random.[1] Whatever may be said about the probability of their occurring, they simply are not effects and hence they do not necessarily happen. In the Free Will philosophy of mind, an answer is first given to the question of whether randomness at the micro-level can give rise to it at the macro-level. The answer given is yes, and so we get random neural events and associated mental events, whatever is subsequently added.

Any discussion of Quantum Theory has to begin with a common distinction that is made in science and in reflection on it. Quantum Theory as the term is often used is in fact two things, a

---

[1]   Quantum Theory is of course not what is called Chaos Theory. The latter has occasionally been taken in recent years as indeterministic, which it is not (Bishop; McFee).

formalism or set of mathematical formulae and an interpretation of that formalism. The interpretation gives you what Quantum Theory comes to in terms of the real world, which may be a lot or a little. Another way of putting it is that the interpretation tells you what the fundamental terms in the theory are to be taken as really meaning or being true of, what their referents are. It is the interpretation that interests us.

The problem of getting to an interpretation has a speculative or in a sense a philosophical character rather than a scientific one. It is a problem to which even solutions of a religious kind have been mentioned, if not taken too seriously. To say the least, there has never been any agreement on this most important matter. This is owed to there being no really clear interpretation available, but many conflicting interpretations—not only the indeterminist sort but also determinist interpretations (Bohm and Hiley; Bohm; Albert; van Frassen; Bub; Cushing; Davies; d'Espagnat; Earman; Omnes; Pagels; Butterfield).

There *is* agreement that such essential and fundamental terms as 'particle' or 'wave' are *not* used as in earlier physics, a physics that was paradigmatically determinist. The same is true of 'position' and 'momentum' and so on. You have only to open a book expounding Quantum Theory for students in order to hear something like this—that in the theory 'familiar concepts . . . take on weird features, or even become meaningless'. This is alarming, and extends to new terms like 'spin', but it is not the main point.

The main point is that there is no really clear interpretation of Quantum Theory, and that this raises a question. What are we supposed to believe? What understanding are we to have of how Quantum Theory applies to the world and to us?

This leads on to second large matter, which can be approached by imagining a little conversation. A universal determinist, someone who applies causation more widely than in his philosophy of mind and action, meets a zealous objector. The objector says that universal determinism is a mistake because not everything is an effect. Numbers aren't effects and propositions aren't effects. In general, what are called *abstract objects* are not effects. He also adds in other sorts of things, perhaps space and time, but let us stick to numbers and propositions.

How will the universal determinist respond? If he has his wits about him, he will be untroubled. He will reply for a start that he never did think that the number 5 was an effect. His theory applies only to *events*, things that happen, and not to abstract objects. There is no sense in trying to refute his determinism by saying about things which he never thought were effects that they aren't effects.

Now to Quantum Theory. It is commonly interpreted as showing that certain things are not effects. What are those things? A certain sort of answer is suggested partly by what is called the Copenhagen Interpretation, perhaps the interpretation that has been foremost. This has much to do with ideas about the consequences for a subject-matter of our experimenting with it or even thinking about it, and indeed ideas about reality being a matter of our own construction. If you read standard expositions of Quantum Theory you can put together a certain list of the things that are not effects. I did that a while ago.

The things that are not effects are: observer-dependent facts, subjective ideas, ideal concepts, contents of our consciousness of reality, propositions, probabilities, features of a calculation, mathematical objects or devices, statistical phenomena, abstract objects, waves in abstract mathematical space, theoretical entities without empirical reality, abstract constructs of the imagination, objects such that statements about them are neither true nor false.

A thought must come to mind immediately. It is that what we ourselves have taken to be effects, events of certain kinds at whatever level, are not what Quantum Theory can be taken to deny are effects. It is at least possible that we can be absolutely untroubled in our determinism. We can certainly say that we must wait for further clarification before there will be need to abandon our theory. It may be that we will have to wait a long time.

It brings a third thing to mind, a simple thing and maybe the largest. Quantum Theory when interpreted in the way that suits Free Will, as you know, says that there are microcosmic events of pure chance, truly random events. They are not necessitated at all, not effects. Is it true?

Well, this interpretation of Quantum Theory has been on the table for about 75 years. In that time, no evidence in a standard sense has been produced for there being any such chance events. *There is no direct and univocal experimental evidence at all.* We have sometimes heard from hopeful science writers in good newspapers that the evidence is on the way from research institutions in

Switzerland or California but it never actually comes. That is really a remarkable fact that needs to be paid attention—75 years is a long time in science.

Someone may say at this point, if he has talked to some physicists, that there is something different that should make us pause, maybe even stop us in our tracks. This is crucial, and it tells in the other direction. It is that Quantum Theory is very successful, an outstanding and paradigmatic scientific theory, and has been for a long time. It works.

One part of this success-story is that it certainly has been accepted by physicists generally. Or rather, it has been accepted if we put aside the unresolved and now wearying confusion about its interpretation. It is accepted when considered as a formalism and also in terms of some experimental results and practical applications. It does fit some experimental data, and it does make some predictions that are confirmed, although this falls well short of direct and univocal experimental evidence. And there are indeed said to be the practical applications, including nuclear reaction, the laser, and so on. Finally, to mention another virtue of the theory, it has been very fertile. It has given rise to new developments.

None of that can be denied, but how much of an argument is it? The real question, so far as we are concerned, is exactly the question of the interpretation of the theory. What does the theory come to in terms of the nature of reality? In fact, the success-story is independent of that, and is not a premise from which an interpretation of the theory follows. It needs to be added that what Quantum Theory replaced was also a greatly successful theory, in the same ways. To boil down this fourth large matter into too short a sentence, the success of a theory is far from being the same thing as the truth of an interpretation or model of a theory.

Fifthly, there would be something to be said even if we conceded that the right interpretation of Quantum Theory is one that conflicts with determinism. It is that it is possible that the real truth about reality will eventually be given by a different physics, one that is deterministic. That remained the conviction of some of the greatest of modern physicists, including Einstein himself. It is not old-fashioned ways that lead to this persisting conviction. Nor, to remember a silly suggestion, is it deep Freudian desires to have a clockwork world. It seems that everything at the macro-level, the level above small particles, which is what we know about best, at least if we put aside the disputed matter of Free Will, is a matter of cause and effect. That must give us a pretty good inductive argument for what is true at the micro-level.

There do exist alternatives to Quantum Theory as indeterministically interpreted, which to a very great extent give the same predictions with respect to observable results (Einstein; Bohm and Hiley; Bohm). These alternatives are to the effect that Quantum Theory is incomplete and that there do exist 'hidden variables', items not taken into account by it, which make for full explanations of all events at the micro-level. The new hidden-variable theories are of course not an attempt to put the clock back to what preceded Quantum Theory, but they are deterministic. They cannot be said to have got much support from orthodox physicists, but it is possible that as I write they are getting rather more. Orthodoxy, in any case, is not to be relied on too much. It is worth remembering that the physics orthodoxy which preceded Quantum Theory seemed to be yet more impregnable.

A sixth matter is the relation touched on a moment ago between the supposed indeterminism at the micro-level and what is true at the macro-level, including the level of neurons. It is often supposed that while there is micro-indeterminism, this is not amplified into indeterminism at the macro-level. Of a number of possible undetermined events at the micro-level, all of them would have the same effect at the macro-level. On the other hand, it is sometimes said, and not always in an attempt to preserve the originator of the Free Will theory, that micro-indeterminism *does* produce indeterminism with respect to the ordinary world.

My own feeling about this is not popular among many physicists, but perhaps it is not too much the worse for that. It is a dilemma for indeterminists. If it is said that indeterminism is true of small particles, but does not get translated into the world we know, including the central nervous system, then we are back where we were. But if it's said on the other hand that micro-indeterminism does produce chance events in the ordinary world, what about the evidence for that? Why have we not noticed one of these chance events? Why has a spoon not levitated before now, when the random lurches of little events within it all happened to combine in the right way?

The common answer made to this is that any levitations, for several reasons, are so totally improbable as in some sense or other to be out of the question. This does not quite satisfy me. If it is true that there is indeterminism in the real world, and finding it would get someone a Nobel Prize, I would have expected a little unquestioned progress by now. *Some* kind of unquestioned progress.

As for the view just mentioned, that there is micro-indeterminism but it leaves everything else determined, including neural events, this is what was earlier called near-determinism, and has sometimes been called naturalism. If it is true, it is identical to determinism in raising the large problem with which we shall soon be concerned—indeed the problem about determinism with which philosophers have been mainly concerned. That is the problem about freedom, responsibility, and so on. The problem therefore does not in fact depend on whether all of our personal existence is a matter of cause and effect. One can be a micro-indeterminist and a macro-determinist, and face the very same problem.

Finally, a couple of thoughts on the opposed philosophy of mind and action in terms of Free Will. We are now in a position to see that it is a mistake to think that it goes well with what it is supposed to depend on, an interpretation of Quantum Theory. We can think of this matter by way of the contradictory idea of a hidden-variable theory of the kind mentioned earlier.

A determinist for obvious reasons may be attracted to such a theory. What is also true is that the Free Will story in a clear sense *is* a hidden-variable theory, if not one to suit a determinist. The Free Will story is that Quantum Theory gives us an undetermined life, with neural and mental events in it that lack explanations, but that something else, an originator, *does* explain these events, thereby making us responsible. That last bit can reasonably be said to be inconsistent with Quantum Theory, which is not supposed to be a partial or incomplete account of reality, including human reality.

Is our theory of determinism then on a level with the Free Will story? Is the short story that both of them conflict with Quantum Theory? That is not a good summary. Our determinism denies an interpretation of Quantum Theory. Free Will, as it seems, has to accept *and* deny that same interpretation. It accepts it in order to escape causation of events. It denies it by then taking those events as *not* chance events. That is not the best of all possible positions. Perhaps Free Will should not try to be up to date.

There is another reason for saying so. Let me finish with a word on a particular marriage of neuroscience and Quantum Theory, familiar and passed by without comment earlier (p. 43), but now performed again by a philosopher who had a good record against Functionalism and the like (Searle 1980, 1992). In an article that is to be followed by a book, Searle has tentatively added Free Will to his previous philosophy of mind, which was inexplicit but which seemed deterministic. What we are now presented with, in my own terms, has to do with the three parts of consciousness— perceptual consciousness, which is seeing and otherwise being aware of things, reflective consciousness, which is thinking of various kinds, and affective consciousness, which has to do with decisions and action and desiring in general.

We are told that your seeing somebody who turns out to be an old friend at a party, say, is caused by a simultaneous neural state. There is that special kind of nomic connection between the two things. The same is true with an item of reflective consciousness, your remembering an instant later that you last parted in anger from your old friend. So too with your consciously deciding in the next minute, after inward turmoil, to go up and apologize, an item of affective consciousness. So in all the three parts of consciousness, we have what we can call down–up causation, simultaneous but otherwise of the standard kind.

As for the coming-about of the first two items in the episode, the earlier event of perceptual consciousness and then the later event of reflective consciousness, causation is the story too with their neural partners. There is standard left–right causation. But our philosopher, in order to be true to his feeling about what are called *gaps* in decision-making processes, has something very different to say when we get to the third item, the decision to apologize. Its neural partner was not the effect of anything at all. Here there is just the chance-relation supposed by the indeterminist interpretation of Quantum Theory—to which, at the conscious level, something as obscure as ever about a Self and explanation by reasons is added.

This is terrible. Down–up causation everywhere in the brain and mind, but just chance or random with some left–right connections. Left–right chance with decisions and more of affective consciousness, but left–right causation with perceptual and reflective consciousness. Down–up causation with respect to decisions but not left–right. The brain and mind are consistently a kind of machine down–up, but not consistently left–right. Sometimes a machine left–right and sometimes not. Our brains and minds jump back and forth between Quantum Theory as indeterministically interpreted and causation, depending on whether we are deciding something or, on the other hand, just seeing or thinking something.

With what respect can be managed, I offer the opinion that this is a kind of dog's breakfast, a kind of factual absurdity. It has no foundation in any respectable neuroscience, I take it. That neuroscience, in accord with our own good sense of reality, supports something else.

Perhaps what most moves me to this unAmerican intemperateness is that there can be no doubt whatever, as we shall soon be seeing in some detail, that certain desires are in play with respect to determinism and freedom. These desires are the stuff of attitudes of hope, moral approval, and so on. They are deep desires, sometimes with religion in them, and they are more in play than desires in some other parts of philosophy. To speak generally, we *want* a certain freedom and the dignity it gives us (Kane), and it seems we want them more as retirement approaches. When suddenly it turns out that an interpretation of Quantum Theory, until now supposed to be a perfectly *general* theory of reality, can be understood as operating in so friendly and local and inconsistent a fashion as to satisfy a philosopher's deep desire, it is possible to wonder, to vary the metaphor, which is the dog and which is the tail.

Do you wonder, reader, if I am failing to tell you of evidence or a good argument supplied by the philosopher in question for his view? Well, what is said is that we are immediately aware of the falsehood of determinism in the course of our daily deciding and acting. We just *experience* its falsehood in the course of any episode of deciding and acting, part of the conscious process. We are aware of 'gaps' in the process. We learn the indeterminist fact from within this stretch of experience, without giving attention to things outside of it.

Whatever else is to be said, this kind of supposition cannot be right as it stands, or very close to right, since it offends against the fact that causal enquiry and causal reasoning are in an essential way general. All clear and arguable accounts of it agree. My conclusion that some event E was the effect of circumstance CC just *is* the conclusion that given CC, whatever else had been happening, E

would still have occurred. My conclusion, then, has to do with other situations of enquiry than this one, often spoken of as counterfactual situations.

Similarly, my more relevant sort of conclusion, say that E was not an effect, not necessitated by any circumstance, is that there was no circumstance such that whatever else had been happening, E would still have occurred. This too is about more situations than this one. In short, any conclusion about determinism or indeterminism and oneself will have to rest on autobiographical reflection rather than some kind of introspection within the experience of deciding and acting as it passes.

There is also a less theoretical consideration. The supposed introspection of an anti-causal or indeterminist fact in our deciding and acting is more than open to question. The various philosophers who declare the existence of this experience, who report on a private delivery of the truth of origination, are in fact engaged in bluff.

Various philosophers on the other side have of course declared as roundly, after the example of John Stuart Mill, that in fact we have *no* experience whatever of gaps in our deciding and acting— supposed absences of causal circumstances. Such things are not the content of our experience at all. What we do have is awareness that our deciding and acting is up to us, in accordance with our own desires, personality, character, etc. (Magill). There is an absence of compulsion, constraint, or any such 'external' causation. What we have, in short, is simply experience of what can be called voluntari-ness, of which you will shortly be hearing a good deal more in another context (chapter 8).

Mill and his fellows might have added something else in analy-sis of our experience, of course. It is that we take our deciding or whatever to have the distinction of being *the cause* in the set of conditions that makes up a causal circumstance for something. This is what is special about deciding and acting as against per-ceiving. This, together with the absence of compulsion, is what lies behind our confidently giving our reason for our action in explanation of why it happened. We do not need the alternative of indeterminism. Nor do we have to think, finally, that in thinking about whether determinism is true, we should pay a lot of attention to our 'consciousness of freedom' as against neuroscience.

There is some other opposition by philosophers to a theory of determinism. It does not have to do with neuroscience and is the subject of the next chapter. We will leave a final conclusion on the truth of our theory to then.

7

SHOTS IN THE FOOT?

THE theory of determinism we have is not a piece of linguistic analysis or detached metaphysics or pure logic. It is a kind of empirical theory. Whether it is true or not depends in the end on the facts. So neuroscience and Quantum Theory and one or two similar things have a large bearing on the question. But these sources of facts are not necessarily all that could have a bearing on it. Philosophers used to be a lot more ambitious in deducing how the world is or isn't, rather than having a look, but they weren't always wrong-headed in this. For a start, a recognizably empirical theory can certainly have conceptual shortcomings, discoverable in an armchair, which get in the way of its being true. Being inconsistent can get in the way of its being true nicely, and inconsistency may be bundled up into something, and hence not on the surface to see.

Those thoughts may well prompt another one. It is that we cannot with perfect ease divide the question of determinism's conceptual respectability from the question of its truth, as we have been trying to do. But let us not linger. What we need to look at are what can rightly be called philosophical objections to the truth of our theory of determinism—they also apply to near-determinism, by the way. We will look at five. They are all to the effect that our theory shoots itself in the foot before getting around to facing the tribunal of the facts.

If the theory is true, each of our futures is somehow predictable. For a start *every* decision and choice to come, however trivial or grave, in some sense can be known now. That has led quite a few people to object that the theory is false. We are *not* able to foretell these things. Quite often the objection focuses on great works of imagination or on scientific achievements. If our theory is true, says the objector, it would have been possible to predict Mozart's music or Einstein's equations the century before, and that is nonsense (Eccles and Popper).

Is it? Well, we need to be clearer about this predictability. Is there a kind of predictability that is nonsense, and a different kind of predictability to which the theory commits us? Certainly a distinction has to be made between what we can just call predictability, and something we can call *conditional predictability*. The distinction is not easy to make sharp.

For something to be predictable is first for someone already to have knowledge about a present thing or state of affairs, or for that knowledge to be recorded, or for it to be gettable. Secondly, this predictability involves causal knowledge, or, as some say, knowledge of laws. You might say knowledge of the way things work. It is because I know that thing is an egg and that other thing is a hammer dropping on it, and because I have some general causal knowledge that applies to eggs and hammers, that it is possible for me to know or have a pretty good idea about the future—that the egg will break.

What is needed for the conditional predictability of something? It is for things to be such that it is conceivable or imaginable for knowledge of them to be had which would enable us to know the future. There *are* things or there *are* facts of the world which if they were known would do the trick. That is not to say that anyone has the knowledge, either of states of affairs or of causal connections, or that this knowledge is recorded, or that it is near to what we ordinarily mean by gettable.

If we make a pretty safe assumption about the regularity of nature, or anyway of the macro-world, it is now in this sense predictable to the millimetre where the last pebble will stop moving at the end of the last avalanche on earth in the twenty-second century. Obviously no one will ever get the requisite knowledge, either of the state of the world at some moment in advance, or of the relevant causal connections. It could even be that causal facts would prevent anyone's ever getting it.

If our theory of determinism is true, then all of each person's future is predictable in this way. If the theory is true, then there are certain facts about past, present, and future. Things *are* such that it is conceivable, however practically impossible, for someone to have knowledge of me mentally and neurally now, and knowledge of environmental effects on me in the future, and knowledge of the necessary causal truths about one sort of thing giving rise to another—which sum of knowledge would enable her to foretell the rest of my life.

Does this logical upshot of our theory provide an argument that the theory is false? I don't think so. Indeed it can seem that someone's opposing the logical upshot doesn't make for an *objection* to the theory at all, but just a plain denial of it expressed in a certain way. This is so since the logical upshot very nearly *is* the theory. To deny the upshot doesn't come to much more than denying the theory. The situation is a little like the one where someone says that he can disprove that you have a new shirt on, and tries to do it just by saying you haven't got a new shirt on. The proposition of conditional predictability is that it is conceivable that someone could know that things are a certain way, and so could say something about the future. That is not far enough from the proposition that things are a certain way.

Still, even if that somewhat puzzling reply works, there is more to be said. We *do* feel a resistance to the thought that someone in a certain sense could predict every bit of our futures. There seems to be something in the jibe about Mozart and Einstein.

Is that because we are rightly totally convinced of the actual impossibility of someone's getting the necessary knowledge, and confusedly transfer our overwhelming sense of this impossibility to the whole proposition that if they had it, they could tell our futures? That sort of habit is very common. It is part of the explanation of our resistance. Clearly it doesn't show that the proposition of conditional predictability is false, any more than the related confusion would falsify the related proposition of conditional predictability about the last pebble in the avalanche.

There is another and larger explanation of our resistance. Rather, we do have another larger kind of resistance. This is not a resistance that involves taking the proposition to be *false*. I can be against something for other reasons than that it is false. This line of thought is important, and will soon be at the centre of our concerns. But it is not about the truth of determinism, but, in a word, about our desires.

Consider a second philosophical objection to the truth of our theory. It is another fantastic supposition or thought-experiment.

Suppose that yesterday a Being predicted how you would choose today in connection with two boxes, and, in accordance with his prediction, he acted in a certain way—of which more in a moment. It might not be wise to identify him with God, but he is along those lines. You can choose today to have both boxes, or to have just the second box by itself. You know the first box definitely contains $1,000. You know the second box contains either $1,000,000 or nothing. You can't see which.

You do know something else. It is that if the Being predicted yesterday that you would be in a way grasping, and choose both boxes, he put nothing in the second box. Also, if he predicted that you would be in a way less grasping and just take the second box, he put $1,000,000 in it. That is not all you know. You also know that the Being has given this choice thousands of times before to other people, and he has never made a mistake in his predictions. Since he has never slipped up, everybody who has chosen to take both boxes has got a lousy $1,000. And everybody who has chosen just the second box has got a cool $1,000,000. Nobody has ever hit the jackpot and got $1,001,000.

That is one side of the story, or the problem, but the other side must not be forgotten. The Being did not merely predict yesterday. He acted. As a result, the second box either has the $1,000,000 in it now or it doesn't.

The problem is of course what you should do. On the assumption that you want to get as much money as possible, do you choose both boxes or only the second one? The problem was devised by a physicist, William Newcomb, and bears his name (Nozick 1970).

Clearly there is a very strong argument for taking just the second box. You might think it is overwhelmingly obvious that that is your best choice. The trouble is that when you think of it, there also seems to be an overwhelming argument for taking both boxes. Either the $1,000,000 is there in the second box or it isn't. There is no question about that. Consider the first possibility, that the money *is* there. Then you must obviously take both boxes, in order to hit the jackpot. Consider the second possibility, that the $1,000,000 *isn't* there. Then you must obviously again take both boxes. That way you will at least get $1,000 rather than nothing. In short, it doesn't matter which thing is true of the second box—you will get $1,000 more by taking both of them.

All of this leads to a further argument against determinism, supplied by a philosopher (Schlesinger 1974, 1976). It runs as follows. Suppose we can convince ourselves that your best choice is to take both boxes. Suppose we can convince ourselves, moreover, that it is just true that by taking both boxes you will end up with the jackpot of $1,001,000. But then we have to admit that the Being will have failed in his prediction. If he had got his prediction right, there wouldn't be money in the second box. This means that there can't be such a thing as we took the Being to be, something that always gets its predictions right. In terms of the earlier distinction, there isn't conditional predictability of choices. But then there can't be determinism either—determinism can't be true. It entails or even asserts conditional predictability. If determinism is true there *would be* this predictability.

What is to be said of this? It may be hard to convince yourself that there is or isn't an argument against determinisn here. But one thing is certain. The argument depends on what is open to doubt, that your right choice is to take both boxes and that you will hit the jackpot. However, I will not try to convince you that your best choice is to take only one box since what seems to me most likely is that Newcomb's Paradox as specified doesn't have a solution. This is so because the situation is left too mysterious and not enough information is given. (Problems don't *have* to have solutions. If a perfectly fair coin is being tossed, and my problem is whether to say heads or tails, there is no solution to that.) What also seems to me likely is that if you change the imagined situation, so that there is a solution to the problem, there isn't an objection to determinism. There is more than one way of changing it.

Suppose we change the imagined situation so that it is natural or possible to think that when people choose both boxes, their choosings actually cause the money in the second box to vanish. We don't have an idea how the causation works, but we think it does. If we think that, there is no problem about what to advise you to do. Don't choose both boxes. And in that case the argument against determinism won't get going.

We might say very differently that the Being can really 'see' into the future, and try to make sense of that. In this case, if we make up our minds that you ought to choose both boxes, maybe we can draw a further conclusion, but it won't be about determinism. It will be that there can't be something that can 'see' into the future, at least not without making mistakes.

Differently again, we might remember that what we were told is that the Being has given the same choice thousands of times before to other people, and he has never made a mistake in his predictions. What does that amount to? What if we think that he is an excellent guesser of personalities and of personal propensities to gamble, but that he has also had a run of luck in his predictions? *If* we think that, then we might advise you to take both boxes. But nothing seems to follow about determinism, since the Being wasn't involved in predicting things on the basis of determinism at all. After all, he might have succeeded in his prediction if he had made use of our theory of determinism.

Here is the most important new thought. We might think that the Being does use premises from determinism. And of course that he never strays from the predictions in which they issue or his regular way of acting on them. He is machine-like. But then if the determinism is true, we know that two things are impossible. It can't happen that somebody chooses both boxes and there is the $1,000,000 in the second. And it can't happen that somebody chooses only the second box and there is nothing in it. So we must advise you to take only the second box. And again, of course, there is no objection to determinism.

Maybe that is not quite right, and it is a little hard to get a hold on. It raises unclear questions. Here is a clearer question. Is *any* argument of this kind for or against determinism likely to cut much ice against empirical evidence for or against determinism?

A third philosophical objection to the truth of our theory of determinism begins from the fact that whenever I have the predictive thought that I am going to do something tomorrow, maybe go to the fine Georgian city of Bath, I can always *step back* from that thought. The same is true if I now think that our theory of determinism is true of me and so I will do something tomorrow. There can be the same stepping-back, the same interrogative or contemplative retreat from the conclusion (Hampshire 1959, 1965, 1972).

The result of this stepping-back is not just a thought or belief that, yes, I will do the thing, or the different prediction that, no, I won't. What I do is make a decision or form an intention. I am not just a spectator of my life, but the real actor in it. When I ask myself the factual question 'What will I do?' this turns into the question 'What should I do?'

But does this fact actually make for an objection to determinism? It is hard to see that it does. For a start, why should my moments of stepping-back not be mental events which are nomic correlates of neural events? Why should these moments not have true of them the rest of what our determinism says of them?

Certainly there is nothing in our theory to the effect that anything that seems to me to have the character or nature of a decision really has the character of just a thought or belief, just a prediction that I will do something. The theory, to be really complete, will have to give an account of the difference between what we naturally call *active* and *passive* mental events, but that is not too hard. The account will have to do with the active ones being according to a plan or directed towards a goal. To return to the main point, though, our theory doesn't turn decisions into just predictions.

Here are the materials of a related fourth objection. Why do I do what I do? A large part of the answer to that question is that I evaluate things, take them to have a value. If you ask me why I am buying these flowers to take home to Ingrid, my explanation cannot leave out something about their being nice or about rooms being bare without flowers, or that it would be a good idea to try to cheer her up after the disaster in the greenhouse. My explanation has some evaluative or normative element. In general our explanations of our own actions have this character.

The objection, as it seems, is that a theory of determinism purports to give a general explanation of actions, and has no evaluative or normative part. If it has no such part, it cannot possibly give a general explanation that is complete. It has to be like our ordinary way of explaining actions (Hampshire 1965).

The reply to the objection must be that while our theory does not include evaluations in one sense, it does in another. It does not actually *make* evaluations, of flowers or anything else, but it certainly takes the making of them into account. It is very far indeed from supposing that high opinions of things, say admiring the looks of someone, do not play a part in bringing about actions. Such mental events are crucial.

Does my ordinary explanation of my own actions differ from this? Well, I will certainly say the flowers are nice or something of the sort when you ask me why I am buying them. But that I bundle things up together in my sentence is not too important. If you press me, I will certainly separate my evaluating from my explaining. What *explains* why I am buying the flowers is the plain true or false proposition—of course I know it is true—that I take them to be nice. It is not the evaluation that they are nice, which seems not to be true or false in the ordinary sense. The two things are not welded together. On the way home I might suddenly get a new low opinion of the flowers, and feel embarrassment at having bought them. I would still say, however shamefacedly, that the explanation of my buying them was that I took them to be nice.

All of the four objections and others like them are to the effect that determinism somehow refutes itself, or anyway can be refuted before we look at neuroscience and the like. The fifth and last objection is yet more explicitly to the effect that determinism shoots itself in the foot, indeed is self-destroying.

It was stated by the ancient Greek philosopher Epicurus, and has been with us ever since. What Epicurus said is that a determinist cannot criticize the doctrine of Free Will because he admits his own criticism is itself determined. He cannot in a real sense object to Free Will because he admits his objection is just a matter of cause and effect. He cannot take what he says to have the respectable standing of real criticism or real objection. The same applies to his own assertion of his own theory and his arguments for it. These too are for him just effects. Furthermore, if the determinist says he *can* really criticize, object, argue for, and so on, this commits him to admitting that his own theory is false. In short, determinism is self-defeating (Chomsky; MacIntyre; Eccles and Popper).

This seems to me the best objection so far, but what does it come to? That is the problem. In fact, different philosophers have made different things of it.

Is the idea that if a judgement is taken to be an effect in the determinist way, it cannot be true? That a determinist cannot take himself really to be arguing because he can't take what he says to be true? That doesn't seem to work. Suppose a judgement's being true consists in its corresponding to a fact. That, after all, is the central definition of what it is for a judgement to be true. There doesn't seem to be any conflict between the judgement's being an effect and its corresponding to a fact.

One scientist first accepted the Epicurean objection to determinism, and then changed his mind (Haldane 1932, 1954). What he first thought was this: 'If my opinions are the result of the chemical processes going on in my brain, they are determined by the laws of chemistry, not logic.' To put the idea in a way many philosophers have, anything that really is an opinion, a judgement, an argument or the like must be owed to Reason, not causation. But what is Reason? There are a lot of answers. Indeed, *all* the versions of the Epicurean objection could be put in terms of Reason. Let us say here that Reason consists in the laws of logic and true propositions generally, where all of those things are abstract objects. But abstract objects don't cause anything. It is no good saying with the scientist that my opinions, if they are to be any good, must be caused by abstract objects. They can't be.

A third idea, all too common, is that if I embrace determinism, I must give up hope of real opinions, arguments, and so on, because my so-called opinions and arguments are effects of just my brain. That is, to go back to something noticed several times, I need to give up arguing if I embrace determinism because determinism comes to epiphenomenalism. But, whatever else is to be said of this particular objection, the theory of determinism we have isn't epiphenomenalism. According to our theory, my opinions *are* partly the effects of my previous opinions, previous mental events.

A fourth idea is better, but how good is it? It runs along these lines. I now have what I think is a true opinion, maybe that determinism is true. According to me, then, that opinion is an effect. But then, it seems, I would have had it whether or not it was true. I would have had it if it were false. What explains my having it is not that it is true, but something else. It may *be* true, but I can have no confidence that it is.

A good reply to this is that it does indeed depend on supposing that if my opinion were false, I would still have been caused to have it. But why should that be the case? If my opinion were false, I might not have been caused to have it. I now think there is a keyboard in front of me. Would I still be caused to think that if there wasn't one? You might say at this point that there is still the argument that causation and confidence can come apart—that causation can't be taken by me to guarantee on every occasion that my opinions are all right. That has to be admitted. But so what? *Nothing* can give me all-encompassing confidence. In particular, I couldn't get it from the doctrine of Free Will.

There is a last and best version of the Epicurean objection, but one that changes its character. It begins from this: that my confidence in having knowledge depends on my being free to do things, or at least my having been free to do things. There is a connection between confidence and action. My confidence that Eric is in the garden cutting the lawn may depend on my being free to go down and check. My confidence in a sentence of this book may depend on my being free to pose certain questions to myself, think of the places where I can find evidence for or against, and so on.

That much has to be granted. It can then go into the following argument. If determinism is true I'm not free, and if I'm not free I can't engage in real investigation or enquiry, and so I can't have confidence either in my opposition to the Free Will philosophy of mind and action or in my support for determinism. This seems to me something to which we have to pay serious attention. But not now. We can best pay attention to it when we turn, as we are about to, to the question of the consequences or implications of determinism.

What remains is a conclusion about the truth of determinism that takes into account neuroscience, Quantum Theory, and what has been considered in this chapter. It should also take into account other science, and also our more ordinary judgements, sometimes called common sense. The conclusion is not that determinism is true. If we suppose that the best that can reasonably be said for any theory is something less than its being true, then our conclusion must be that determinism does not quite get that lesser honour. The conclusion that in my opinion we do need to draw was anticipated earlier. It is that taking in account everything, determinism is *very strongly supported*, and that certainly it has *not been shown to be false*. It will be no news to you that I myself *do* think determinism is true, but that thought does seem even to me to go a bit beyond the evidence.

If we take just the conclusion that determinism has not been shown to be false, there is the problem of its consequences. What follows if it is true? There is the same question, of course, if we are near-determinists. If we believe in what was called micro-indeterminism, but think it does not issue in macro-indeterminism, but rather leaves neural and mental events a matter of cause and effect, we also have to think in just the same way about what determinism comes to for our lives.

8

DISMAY, INTRANSIGENCE

W E hope for a lot of things, most of them small. We hope to get home by 7 o'clock for the news on television, that someone won't be annoyed by what was said last night, that it will be sunny on Sunday. More important, we also hope for large things, for what can be described as one large thing. A young woman hopes above all to become an actress. She holds to this hope and guides herself by it and does all she can to realize it. Others preserve their hope to get some other kind of standing or respect, or to possess something, perhaps a home of a certain kind. I may hope to succeed in a long struggle against my competitors, or to come to have a kind of relationship with another person, or to avoid a disaster. Someday I may mainly hope to delay death.

Hopes for large things can be given the name of *life-hopes*. Such a hope gives to an individual's life a good deal of its inside nature. Different such hopes mark the stages of a life. It is such a hope that at any time provides or rather *is* an individual's attitude to his or her future. To contemplate my future now, my coming life, is to have such a hope. It would of course be mistaken to suggest that each life-hope has sharp definition or is for some single thing, as in the examples so far. A life-hope can be vaguer, as when someone wants life to turn out decently, or not to get worse. It can be for a few large things rather than one. The thing or things will be large in terms of the individual's life, but not necessarily regarded as large by others. We can be so unlucky as to hope above all for just enough to eat. That is the prospect we want, what we feel will satisfy us.

Life-hopes seem in general to have two kinds of content. There is a state of affairs that we hope for—say being regarded as in some way a success, or the family's being in good shape, or just owning a car. The state of affairs in this narrow sense is important, but less important than something else. The other kind of content of a hope has to do with our future actions, maybe a long campaign of them.

What this comes to in one part is that we want not just to have things, but to achieve them. The state of affairs of being regarded as a success is one thing, and having earned it is another. But even if we are not self-examining strivers focused in this way on doing things for ourselves, our hopes will have everything to do with our future actions. That is because we rightly believe that it is only, mainly, or importantly through our own actions that we will get what we want. Even if what I want is to be rich, and I do not much mind how that comes about, I will take it that my getting rich will depend on what I do. We are not fatalists of a certain ancient kind, who feel that what will happen in their futures will have nothing to do with their own actions. At any rate we do not ordinarily think or feel this way. We think of our futures in terms of our coming actions. In particular, we think in terms of what can be called *initiating* our actions.

You might ask at this point what a hope is. A short answer is that a hope is an attitude to the future. And what in general is an attitude? It is worth giving an answer to this general question. Our coming reflections, although they will not all be about life-hopes, will all be about attitudes.

You can say that an attitude is an evaluative thought of something, which is to say an approving or disapproving thought, where the thought is bound up with desire, and somehow feelingful. If we think of certain examples of attitudes rather than others, more pressing ones, it may seem better to start by saying an attitude is a desire rather than a thought, but the same elements will come in. An attitude is like an intention in that it has various elements. It is also like an emotion in this way. As for the distinction between an attitude and an emotion, an emotion is likely to be more transient and involve more excited feeling.

Any attitude, then, takes something to be good or bad, and involves desiring it or not, and brings in feelings. The latter are somehow related to sensations. The feelings are prominent in some cases, notably a fearful attitude. To get back to hope, we can now say a bit more than that it is an attitude to the future. A hope is a desire for something, involving an approving valuation of it, bound up with feeling, and such that it is not certain that the thing will come about.

The main thing about life-hopes, and about all the other attitudes we will be considering, is that they come in two kinds or families. That is not to say that some individuals have one kind and other individuals the other, but that each of us has or can have both kinds. The difference between them has to do with the thoughts of our future actions that enter into them, and at bottom thoughts about what was called the initiation of those actions. A young woman can have a life-hope to be an actress which involves her future actions thought of by her as having one sort of initiation— and also a life-hope to be an actress where her actions are thought of by her as having the other sort of initiation.

Life-hopes of the first kind, to speak of them in one way, partly involve thinking of our futures as open or unfixed or alterable. If I have a hope of this kind, I take it that questions about my future are not yet answered—it is not that the answers are already settled and stored up, but that they do not yet exist. I've got a chance. It's up to me. Maybe I can succeed. I am not the kind of fatalist committed to the argument that just since it is true now that this or that will happen next year, it is settled now that it will happen. We aren't fatalists of this kind. One piece of evidence is that when philosophers turn their attention to this fatalism, their purpose is always to try to refute the argument, since they take its conclusion that everything is settled to be false.

Life-hopes of this first kind can be spoken of in another way. They can be said to involve thinking that our futures are not just products or automatic upshots. They will not just be products of our characters, weaknesses, temptations, and so on—in short, our natures. Also, our futures will not be just products of our natures taken together with the situations in which we will find ourselves. I will not drink more and more, and nor will I be the toy of my circumstances, a leaf in the breeze.

This first kind of life-hope, spoken of in either of the two ways, carries some impression of activity, something that can change things, and can rise above the rest of a person's nature and environment. You may by now have guessed what is coming. It is the idea that life-hopes of this first kind are related to the philosophical account of persons in terms of Free Will or origination.

That is not to say that these hopes are near to containing a conception of an unchanging substance sailing through time or a worked-out doctrine of Free Will. They contain no such thing, but rather a kind of impression or image. It is this that philosophers have turned into a doctrine. It is safe to say that the impression comes before the philosophy.

So I do have or can have this kind of life-hope with respect to my future. It also has in it an image of my future actions as being initiated in a certain way: they will be something like originated. That is what makes the future open, and my nature and environment overcomable. These actions in my present anticipation of them will almost certainly have another character, of course. They will really be mine in the sense that they will not be against either my wishes or my true nature. We will come on to that separate and important idea about their initiation, but let us pause for a moment to deal with a possible doubt, a doubt about the existence of this first kind of life-hope.

Does anyone really doubt having or being able to have this kind of very natural hope? If so, they can stop doubting by contemplating what it would be like really not to have it. What it would be like not to have this hope would be to feel that you were in something which William James, the brother of the novelist, called the iron-block universe. That is, the universe of which universal determinism is true. This determinism, James wrote,

professes that those parts of the universe already laid down appoint and decree what other parts shall be. The future has no ambiguous possibilities hidden in its womb; the part we call the present is compatible with only one totality. Any other future complement than the one fixed from eternity is impossible. The whole is in each and every part, and welds it with the rest into an absolute unity, an iron block, in which there can be no equivocation or shadow of turning.

We do hope otherwise, which is to say not just that we accept the iron-block universe but that we add something to it. We have a hope which does not go with the iron-block universe at all. We have a kind of life-hope which is incompatible with a belief in determinism, either the theory in this book about persons or a universal one. An open future, a future we can make for ourselves, *is* one of which determinism isn't true.

Suppose you become convinced of the truth of our theory of

determinism. Becoming really convinced will not be easy, for several reasons. But try now to imagine a day when you do come to believe determinism fully. Also imagine bringing your new belief together with a life-hope of the kind we have been considering, this natural way of contemplating your future. What would the upshot be? It would almost certainly be *dismay*. Your response to determinism in connection with the hope would be dismay. If you really were persuaded of determinism, the hope would collapse.

This is so because such a hope has a necessary part or condition on which the rest of it depends. That is the image of origination. There can be no such hope if all the future is just effects of effects. It is for this reason, I think, that many people have found determinism to be a black thing. John Stuart Mill felt it as an incubus, and, to speak for myself, it has certainly got me down in the past.

The response of dismay in connection with life-hopes has to do with one kind of them. There is another kind. We can also approach it by seeing what it is like to lack it. Think of a man who has lost his job, and whose life-hope is therefore waning or has been lost. The future he wanted was one with a job. He hoped for more of the kind of life he had in the past, one that goes with having a job. In particular, he had in mind being independent, being regarded in a certain way by his children, being active, and having the things that come with decent pay. Now, there is little or nothing left of that hope.

What does he feel? What he feels is that he will continue to be frustrated in his desire. The world, or anyway the world of work, will continue to be against him. He will have to put up with the drudgery of watching too much television, or whatever else goes into the place of what he would rather do. His life will be one of acting on or satisfying only what we can call reluctant or second-best desires, as distinct from *embraced desires*, desires into which he really enters. He will live in a frustrating world, not a satisfying one.

To turn now to luckier people, they can and do have hopes that have in them the picture of future actions done out of embraced and not reluctant desires. They are not always hopes that have to do with not being frustrated by a world, where that is a matter of a whole society or the state of it. We may have hopes that have to do with not being frustrated by ourselves. What I may want above all is to escape some personal weakness or self-indulgence or habit that drags me down. I myself may have desires which go against and overcome my embraced desire. I would rather not have them. I drink too much, or don't get down to work. More dramatically I may be the victim of an addiction to hard drugs or a psychological compulsion. I want to live differently (cf. Frankfurt 1969).

If my hopes of this kind may have to do with my future actions and either my world or myself, they may also have to do with my actions and a few other people. My hope may be to escape the domination or influence of others. More dramatically, it may be to escape from a real threat. In most of our lives, that is unlikely to involve a man with a gun, more likely to be one of the respectable threats of ordinary or business life. Or, finally, my hope may have to do with escaping some particular physical constraint. I want not to be sick, or to have a bodily disability, or to be in jail.

So here we have a kind of hope that brings in actions owed to a certain kind of initiation, different from before. These are actions flowing just from embraced rather than reluctant desires, actions done in satisfying and not frustrating circumstances. Such an action, as we can also say, reverting to something said earlier, really does come from an individual—it is not against his or her desires or true nature. To introduce a label, its initiation is a matter of *voluntariness*. We can think of an action in just this way, without adding in anything else, any different idea. We can have hopes involving actions conceived in just this way. The man without a job once had a hope, and maybe now has the remainder of one, which is fully described in the way we have described it. His spirits will soar if he is just offered the chance to do what he wants, to work. He will be satisfied by exactly that.

If we now bring hopes of this second kind together with determinism, what is the result? Our response will be owed to what is certainly a fact, that determinism can be true without affecting these hopes at all. There is nothing in them that is inconsistent with it. There is nothing about embraced desires and satisfying situations that conflicts with determinism. Working because I really want to and because I think of nothing else is just as consistent with determinism as watching television reluctantly. To use the label, there is nothing about actions being voluntary in their initiation that conflicts with determinism. For determinism, voluntary actions are ones that have a certain kind of causal history, as distinct from any non-causal history. Voluntary actions are effects of a certain class.

Our response to thinking of determinism together with this kind of hopes will mainly be that the hopes are untouched and untroubled. Everything is okay. Nothing changes. Our response may also involve a thought about hopes of the other sort—and our disregarding them as unimportant. We may feel we don't have to think about them. This response as a whole involves rejecting dismay. This way with determinism is a kind of satisfied intransigence.

I do not mean to suggest that the two kinds of life-hope and the two responses to determinism are always exactly as described. What has been said is schematic and without shading. In reality there is a lot more variation and complexity. But it does seem a fact that each of us has or can have an attitude to the future involving an image of origination, as well as ideas of voluntariness, and an attitude involving only ideas of voluntariness, and that each of us at least can make the two reponses. That does not have to be a law of human nature for my argument, just a fact about most of us.

Neither kind of attitude to the future, considered in itself, can be regarded as any kind of mistake. There is no room for the idea of mistake. I *can* regard or take just my anticipated voluntariness as a reason for a feeling about the future. I *can* at another time take only an anticipation of my also being able to originate my actions as a reason for a feeling about the future. It is a fact too that responding with intransigence or dismay involves no mistake in itself. There is more to be said about these responses, but nothing that will take away from the fact that they are possible and indeed natural.

There is the same story with other things than life-hopes. Although these other pairs of attitudes are best described a little differently in each case, the fundamental facts are the same. Generally speaking, we have attitudes that have to do only with actions taken as really owed to the agents or actors, not against either their desires or their true natures, and we have attitudes having to do with actions taken as really owed to the agents but also originated.

Consider certain attitudes we have to other people. These we can call the personal feelings (P. F. Strawson). They are of the greatest importance to our lives. There are positive or appreciative ones owed to the good feelings of others for us, and the good judgements of others on us, and their resulting actions towards us. Our lives as we live them are tremendously the better for the love, loyalty, and acceptance of others, and for their approval and admiration, and what they do out of all these feelings. There are also our negative or resentful personal feelings. These are also owed to the attitudes of others towards us, in this case their feelings and judgements against us, and the resulting actions. Our resentful feelings, from hatred down to pique, do not enrich our lives, but they are rooted in them. It is hard to imagine life without them, or to feel confident about escaping them.

The personal feelings are not moral feelings, although they may be mixed up with them. I can be grateful for something you have done without thinking of it as right or wrong, or of you as getting or losing moral credit for it. I may even be grateful for a good review of my book which I know was not a masterpiece of impartiality. So too with my resentful feelings. I may not be able to succeed in what I will no doubt try to think, that you did wrong in hurting me, but that is no guarantee that I will like you.

Suppose I come to believe that someone, an adversary, has tried to pay me back for something by a certain means. He has reported a story of a careless, wounding comment of mine to the man it was about, a friend on whom I depend. This will be of no benefit at all to me. The report of what I said, if a bit overdone, had truth in it. I resent, no doubt more than resent, the carrier of the tale. What does my feeling involve?

I may say in expressing my bitterness that he could have done otherwise. And I may fill that in by saying various things. He knew what he was doing, his report wasn't just a slip. Also, he wasn't compelled to do the thing, perhaps out of control and actually carried away by passions. Thirdly, I do not think the action was wholly out of character, really at odds with his personality. He himself, I say, is malicious or vengeful, or anyway not honourable. I may add that he is not mad either, but normal enough, with an adequate sense of the hurts of other people. I may point out, finally, that nobody else was part of his action. He was not being manipulated or the like.

These are all assumptions or beliefs about the initiation of my adversary's action. They are assumptions like some of those I may make about my own future actions in connection with one kind of my hopes. What we have here is what was labelled voluntariness, and no more than that. It is clear that all the assumptions are consistent with determinism. It does not at all follow from determinism that a man does not really know what he is doing, or is compelled to do a thing, or is unusual in any of the other ways touched on above. It doesn't follow from determinism that a man couldn't do otherwise than he did, where that means he didn't know the facts, or was compelled to do the thing, or the like. There is the same fact, by the way, about personal feelings that have not been mentioned, personal feelings directed not towards others but towards oneself.

Thinking of these personal feelings, and supposing determinism to be true, again may issue in the response of intransigence. We can take determinism to leave things just as they are. We do not feel called on to do the humanly impossible, to withdraw from these resentful feelings. We do not lose the satisfaction of the appreciative feelings. If there are other grounds for another kind of personal feelings, grounds that are threatened by determinism, we can ignore the matter. What we have is enough.

That is all very well, but I can also think and react differently, and not necessarily on another day or in another mood. This can come about in various ways. I may come to feel in connection with my adversary that my bitterness is or has to be directed against a *person*. It cannot just be concerned with a bundle of facts, features of a person, starting with something about a state of knowledge, going on to something about control or the absence of compulsion, then something about character, and so on. *He* carried the tale to my friend.

Here is a stronger thought going in the same direction. I may be faced by someone with excuses and explanations of my adversary's action. Someone will say that he could hardly have resisted the temptation of striking that little blow by telling the story. At this point I am certain to feel and to say that in a fundamental way he could have resisted the temptation. He could have resisted it even if it had been strong. He could have done otherwise, where that does not just mean that he knew what he was doing, he wasn't out of control, and so on. He could have done otherwise in the sense that given things as they were, strong temptation and all, he could have done differently.

These reflections and others like them can lead me to think of his action differently. I turn from thinking of it as merely voluntary to thinking of it as also owed to him himself. My bitterness carries the image of his having originated what he did. This kind of personal feeling *does* conflict with determinism. If determinism is true, I am likely to feel I have to give it up, and all attitudes like it. I also need to give up something a lot happier, the counterpart kind of appreciative attitudes to other people. Gratitude, what I may think of as real gratitude, has to go. This is the response of dismay with respect to personal feelings. I may move back and forth between it and intransigence. Certainly I *can* fall into it.

There is no mistake and nothing to stop me from taking just the thought of a fully voluntary action as a reason for a feeling, and no mistake or anything that stops me from also requiring an originated action for a feeling. I can focus on one conception of the initiation of action or the other, with the two upshots. This will be important when we come, as we shall soon, to what were mentioned at the beginning of this book, the traditional doctrines of Compatibilism and Incompatibilism.

Determinism does not have consequences for only life-hopes and personal feelings. It has a third consequence, of which we already know something. It has to do with knowledge, and is what is really important about the Epicurean objection to determinism. More precisely, it has to do with our confidence in having knowledge, a kind of attitude to ourselves. What it has to do with is the fact that knowledge is owed to enquiry, and enquiry consists in actions, above all the mental activity of trying to answer questions and solve problems.

Here we can think of our own personal enquiries, or the large joint enterprise over centuries which brought together our shared conceptual scheme and our general view of things. I can have an idea of any enquiry as being the discovery of reality, with none of its sectors closed off. This is exploration, not a guided tour. The picture includes an image of origination. Alternatively, I can have the idea of enquiry as only a matter of myself or others not being frustrated in any desire for information. Neither circumstances nor people get in the way. Here the picture rests only on voluntariness. In short, I can have two different ideas of freedom in enquiry.

These two attitudes to reality, or kinds of confidence about reality, stand in relations to determinism that you will anticipate. I am unlikely on any occasion to persist long in the attitude including origination. But to have it in mind is to have something in mind that must give way to determinism. That is depressing. It is depressing to suppose there may be a reality other than the one to which a guided tour fixed by causation has restricted me. With the attitude involving only voluntariness, I may take it that determinism carries no threat at all. There is no ground for serious worry.

We have now seen something of three things touched by determinism—our life-hopes or contemplated futures, our personal feelings, and our knowledge. It may be, as I suspect, that these three areas of consequence are the most important. Certainly they cannot be left out. We are unlikely to come to any true judgement about the consequences of determinism if they are ignored. Philosophers have in fact ignored them, which may help to explain why no agreement has ever been reached about the import of determinism for our lives.

What philosophers have until now thought about, with one or two honourable exceptions, is just a fourth implication of determinism, the implication for moral responsibility. Certainly it needs thinking about, as do three other related implications. These in a way depend on our thoughts and feelings about moral responsibility. They have to do with what is right or what actions are right, and with the moral standing of individuals, and with the social institutions and practices such as punishment which result from these conceptions.

We will come back to punishment and the like. For now, just consider moral responsibility. The subject-matter is sometimes left or made obscure, but it comes to holding people (including ourselves) morally responsible for something bad, and crediting people (including ourselves) with moral responsibility for something good. These again are attitudes we have. What they come to, differently described, is being morally disapproving of a person in connection with an action, and being morally approving of a person in connection with an action.

Again, these attitudes fall into two kinds, and each of us has both. In this case there seems little need for weakening the claim by saying that at least we *can* have both. If a man injures my daughter in the street, or defrauds her in a financial transaction, or concocts evidence against her in a court, I can focus on his action as voluntary but also originated. I hold him responsible where that involves my seeing his action in a certain way. It came out of his own desires and the person he is, *and* it was such that he could have stopped himself from doing it given things as they were. My holding him responsible also involves my having certain feelings and desires. In particular, I have a *retributive desire*. I want it to come about that he suffers at least some unhappiness about what he has done. The desire may go a lot further than that.

Now, to proceed a little differently from life-hopes and so on, suppose not that I become convinced on some future day of the theory of determinism we have been considering, but just that right now I fall into a common kind of half-determinist feeling and thinking about his action. This sort of thing often has to do with thoughts of the underprivileged background and history of a person. I come to feel that given the sort of person he is, and given the situation he was in, he did not have much chance of behaving differently. What happens? My retributive desire at least falters. Alternatively, suppose I am at the pitch of my feeling against him, and someone else courageously or unwisely pleads the story of his background and history to me. My reaction may be a determination to persist in my vengeful feeling by denying or questioning the half-determinist story.

What these reflections show is that holding someone responsible can be something that is inconsistent with determinism. To think of this way of holding people responsible, and to contemplate that determinism is true, is to face dismay. This is partly so since we are required to give up a feeling that we rightly take to be deeply rooted in us. There is the same result, perhaps in a way more troubling, with crediting others and ourselves with responsibility for good or estimable actions.

That is not the end of the matter. There is no doubt that I can in another way hold the injurer of my daughter responsible. I can focus just on the fact that the injury he did to her was voluntary. It was really owed to him and to his own desires. I can enlarge on this fact to myself in various ways. I can without doubt have strong feelings about him, and speak of his voluntariness as the reason. They will include feelings of repugnance for this person who was able to do the thing in question, and desires for the prevention of more such injuries. There is the same possibility in the different case where I morally approve of someone.

Will anyone doubt all this? Well, a kind of doubt has been raised as to whether we ordinary folk and the philosophers of origination have *any* half-adequate idea of origination at all. Certainly the philosophers of origination have not been able to do well at clarifying their commitment (see chapter 4). And it can hardly be maintained that our ordinary attitudes have more than a kind of impression or image in them (p. 94). But is it only some piece of nonsense, such as the old nonsense of speaking of a thing causing itself?

If so, what has just been said of our two families of attitudes is a great mistake. We only have one family of attitudes that deserves the name. And a certain dispute over centuries between two doctrines mentioned in the first chapter of this book, Compatibilism and Incompatibilism, has been a perfectly pointless one between something sensible and a nonsense. Furthermore, to look back to chapters 6 and 7, it does not matter if determinism is true or false, since there is no serious idea with which it conflicts. The question of its truth does not need looking into. That was time wasted (G. Strawson).

This is a surprising position. There is some bravado in supposing that reflective persons have for some centuries been involved in close dispute about only a nonsense. It is possible to think otherwise. As remarked earlier, the fact seems to be that we all have a primitive idea of the initiation of decisions and actions such that they are not just effects but are controlled by the person in such a way that he or she can be held responsible in a certain way—and such that life-hopes and other related attitudes are also possible (pp. 93–4).

Consider a parallel. Suppose I have no idea of why the sweet peas in the garden *need sun*, but am persuaded they do, no doubt by good evidence. Despite the evidence, I have no acquaintance at all with photosynthesis, not even any boy's own science of the matter. It does not follow, presumably, that I lack the idea that the sweet peas *need sun*. I could have the idea, too, in a pre-scientific society where news of the science of the thing would for a long time make no sense. Could I not also have the idea, in a later society, if all of many attempts to explicate the need had broken down in obscurity and indeed contradiction?

At first sight, certainly, those who suppose that there *is* a half-adequate idea of origination are in just this sort of position. They speak no nonsense when they assert or offer for contemplation a certain thing. It is that there occur originations, these being events that are not effects, are in the control of the person in question, and render the person responsible in a certain way for ensuing actions—his being held responsible can consist in an attitude having in it certain desires, notably retributive ones. The friends of origination speak no nonsense when they depend considerably for their characterization of the events of origination on these consequences. The friends have still spoken no nonsense when it transpires that they cannot in some way explain how it comes about that there is origination, or would come about if there were any. They have still spoken no nonsense if their attempts to explain are themselves pieces of nonsense.

Maybe more distinctions are needed here—they usually are—but it certainly remains my own view that determinism *does* threaten something important to us.

There *is* the broad fact that each of us has or can have two families of attitudes, one having to do with actions taken as owed to voluntariness or the desires and natures of the agents, and one taken as also owed to origination. We have or can have two kinds of life-hope, two kinds of confidence in knowledge, two kinds of personal feeling, and two kinds of moral feeling about people and their actions. Something of the same sort is to be said about taking actions to be right or wrong, and having general judgements of people not in connection with a single action.

There is also the equally important broad fact that we can make two responses to determinism, Dismay and Intransigence. We can take determinism as destructive and we can take it as harmless. We can take is as a black thing and we can take it as just a tolerable background fact.

Something follows immediately from the proposition of *Attitudinism*, that we have the two kinds of attitudes, and the proposition about responses to determinism. These propositions must bear on the two doctrines just mentioned, Compatibilism and Incompatibilism. That is our next subject.

The two propositions also give rise to a large problem. Is there more to be said for one of the responses of Dismay and Intransigence than the other? Is there very much to be said for either? Is there more to be said for a third response? We will get to that.

9

COMPATIBILISM AND INCOMPATIBILISM

PHILOSOPHY in the English language has mainly been clear, cool, and more or less in touch with common sense and the facts of science. It has not gone in much for either high reasoning or deep thinking, which inclinations are stronger in French and German philosophy. David Hume of the eighteenth century is the patron saint of the main kind of philosophy in English. In one respect, though, he is usually given some credit that is better given to his predecessor, Thomas Hobbes of the seventeenth century. Hobbes can be regarded as the first of the Compatibilists. Perhaps he had predecessors, but he was the first of the great philosophers to propound the proposition of Compatibilism. It is that determinism and freedom are logically consistent, that our concept of freedom is such that we can be subject to determinism and also perfectly free.

This is not the proposition that determinism is consistent with Free Will or origination, that we can both originate choices and also be subject to causal necessity. The idea, rather, is that what we mean by *freedom*, which in fact is not Free Will, is compatible with determinism. Incompatibilism, the opposed tradition, is that what we mean by freedom is not compatible with determinism since part of what we mean *is* Free Will.

We need to look at this long battle for two reasons. One is that it contrasts with what has just been argued about two families of attitudes and two responses. The contrast makes that argument and the conclusions clearer. The second reason is that these two philosophical traditions make up the opposition to a view of this book about the consequences of determinism—and of course near-determinism. The view may not be right, as I have taken it to be, but it is certainly new and can do with more clarifying. What we have arrived at about attitudes and responses is the first part of it. If what the opposition parties say is right, Attitudinism and what has been said about responses to determinism can't be true.

Hobbes asks what liberty or freedom is, and gives this answer:

> there can no other proof be offered but every man's own experience, by reflection on himself, and remembering what he uses in his mind, that is, what he himself means when he says an action . . . is free. Now he that reflects so on himself cannot but be satisfied . . . that a *free agent* is he that *can do as he will,* and *forbear as he will,* and that *liberty* is *the absence* of *external impediments.* But to those that out of custom speak not what they conceive . . . and are not able or will not take the pains to consider what they think when they hear such words, no argument can be sufficient, because experience and matter of fact are not verified by men's arguments but by every man's own sense and memory.

What this comes to is that if you'll just think about it, you'll see that what you and all of us mean by being free is being able to act in a certain way if that is what we want, and not to act in that way if that is what we want. Being unfree is being frustrated, being stopped from doing whatever we want by external impediments. That is the idea we all have, as each of us can find out by remembering it and thinking about it.

Hobbes in other passages emphasizes what is certainly clear, that we can be free in this way even if determinism or what he calls *necessity* is a fact, which he is sure it is. He also emphasizes that this freedom is exactly what is required if we are to hold people morally responsible and credit people with moral responsibility for what they do.

Bishop Bramhall thought otherwise in his not entirely calm reply to Thomas Hobbes. He said in part that Hobbes's freedom or liberty, which amounts to not being frustrated, is no great thing. It is not to be confused with true liberty.

> true liberty consists in the elective power of the rational will. . . . Reason is the root, the fountain, the original of true liberty. . . . Judge then what a pretty kind of liberty it is which is maintained by T.H., such a liberty as in little children before they have the use of reason, before they can consult

or deliberate of anything. Is not this a childish liberty, and such a liberty as in brute beasts, as bees and spiders . . . ? Is not this a ridiculous liberty? Lastly (which is worse than all these) such a liberty as a river has to descend down the channel. . . . Such is T.H.'s liberty. . . . T.H. appeals to every man's own experience. I am contented. Let everyone reflect upon himself.

In short we all know that freedom or liberty is not had by animals, although they can often do what they want, or by rivers, which are not frustrated in running down their channels. Freedom, as we all know if we think about it, is a matter of adult Reason. It is a matter, more precisely, of the developed Faculty of the Will or the power of origination.

Bishop Bramhall did not convince Hobbes, and he did not convince Hume either. Hume took the view that disagreements about things we all know about can only continue if the disagreements involve ambiguous terms.

This has been the case in the long disputed question concerning liberty and necessity, and to so remarkable a degree that, if I am not much mistaken, we shall find that all mankind, both learned and ignorant, have always been of the same opinion with regard to this subject, and that a few intelligible definitions would immediately have put an end to the whole controversy.

Hume then proceeds to what he calls his reconciling project. If we think straight about it, we can agree that what we mean by liberty or freedom is

a power of acting or not acting, according to the determinations of the will: that is, if we choose to remain at rest, we may; if we choose to move, we also may. . . . This hypothetical liberty is universally allowed to belong to everyone who is not a prisoner and in chains. Here, then, is no subject of dispute.

Hume's use of the word 'power' has nothing to do with the mysterious power of origination talked of by the defenders of Free Will. Being free is just having power in the sense that you can do what you want—your wants give rise to what happens, not prison chains or the like. Having this power is perfectly possible even if determinism is true, as Hume thinks determinism is. Determinism does not say there are never internal causes of actions, actions really owed to the agent. Also, a person's having this power and nothing else is all that is needed in order to be responsible for actions and to be rightly punished for them.

Immanuel Kant, the great German philosopher, was not at all persuaded.

Suppose I say of a man who has committed a theft that this act by the natural law of causality is a necessary result of the determining ground existing in the preceding time and that it was therefore impossible that it could have not been done. . . . How can he be called free . . . ? It is a wretched subterfuge to seek an escape in the supposition that the kind of determining grounds of his causality according to natural law agrees with a comparative concept of freedom. According to this concept, what is sometimes called 'free effect' is that of which the determining natural cause is internal to the acting thing. . . . With this manner of argument many allow themselves to be put off and believe that with a little quibbling they have found the solution to the difficult problem which centuries have sought in vain and which could hardly be expected to be found so completely on the surface.

What we do and must understand by the term 'freedom', according to Kant, is not action caused by something internal rather than external to the agent. It is 'spontaneous origination', not subordinate to causality at all. All of us, unless we are taken in by the quibbling, see that this conviction of ours is exactly this that is required to explain another fact, that we are certainly morally responsible for our actions.

To come quickly to the middle of the twentieth century, the Cambridge philosopher G. E. Moore took the view that whatever else we mean by saying an action was free, we partly mean that the person in question could have done otherwise. Moore then set to work to analyse what it is to say a person could have done otherwise. He decided it is to say something like this: she would have done otherwise if she had wanted to. But then she could have done otherwise even if determinism is true. Determinism doesn't say that she wouldn't have done otherwise than she did if she had wanted to do that other thing. She might then have done the other thing, since there would have been a different cause operating. Moore therefore cautiously embraced Compatibilism.

The Oxford philosopher J. L. Austin also did some neat work on what it means to say a person could have done otherwise. He showed to his satisfaction that it doesn't mean what Moore had in mind, that if there had been a different cause operating, the person would have done otherwise. It doesn't mean anything about causes. To say an effect Y would have happened if its cause X had happened, it seems, is to say Y wouldn't have happened without X. But to say a person could have done otherwise if she'd wanted *is* to say she might have done otherwise even though she didn't want to. Austin therefore cautiously embraced Incompatibilism.

Both Austin and Moore, by the way, held back from deciding whether or not determinism is true. There have been many other such Compatibilists and Incompatibilists. The question they ask is not 'Since determinism is true, what then?' but 'If determinism is true, what then?' As for the dispute between Moore and Austin about 'could have done otherwise', we need not get into that. We do need to notice one thing. Moore and Austin do agree that we all mean one thing when we talk about freedom, and one thing when we say a person could have done otherwise.

The long battle between Compatibilists and Incompatibilists has carried on since the time of Moore and Austin. Philosophical journals do not leave it alone for long. Books keep coming out. Proofs are announced. Fuller and better accounts of what we are supposed to mean by 'free' are given by Compatibilists. They improve on Hobbes and Hume by including in the story something about an absence of internal impediments as well as of external impediments, and also something to keep spiders and rivers out of it, and so on.

We will come back to some of this, but already we have a summary of the main things believed by the two sides, who are partly in agreement.

1. They agree that we all share some single settled idea of what has to be true of a choice if it counts as free, and hence of what has to be true of an action if it counts as free. They say this single concept about the initiation of choices, since we all agree on it, is written into our language.

2. Compatibilists say that our single settled idea of a free choice is of a choice that is according to the desires of the chooser. It is what the chooser really wants. So with a free action. A free choice or action is essentially what was labelled a voluntary one in the last chapter: it is according to the agent's desires and true nature, not against them. Incompatibilists disagree and say that what we all

think is a free choice is not only one that the chooser in his true nature really wants but also one that is owed to Reason or the Faculty of the Will or whatever. A free choice is a voluntary *and* an originated one.

3. Both sides agree in assigning to all of us a certain belief, which they take to be a plain truth. It is the factual belief that something is necessary for something else. A free choice is necessary for holding the person responsible. The sides differ, as just remarked, about what we are all supposed to take a free choice to be.

4. Incompatibilists say, as a result, that we all know that people are only morally responsible if determinism is false. Only then can there be choices that are both voluntary and originated. Compatibilists say differently that we all know that people can be perfectly morally responsible even if determinism is true. All we need for responsibility is a voluntary choice.

5. Both sides agree that the question they are concerned with is a logical or intellectual or theoretical one. What we have to do is just see clearly, not get confused, get a good definition of the idea we all share, not get led astray by other philosophers with a doctrinal axe to grind, check what is or isn't consistent with what, pay attention to this or that proof of what freedom involves. The question is importantly a linguistic one. What we have to do is analyse 'free' in ordinary English and similar words in other ordinary languages.

Neither the tradition of Compatibilism nor the tradition of Incompatibilism is absolutely uniform. There are differences between philosophers in the same tradition. John Stuart Mill is not exactly the same as Hobbes, Hume, and Moore, and Jean-Paul Sartre is not exactly the same as Bishop Bramhall, Kant, and Austin. Still, it is safe to say that in the five propositions above we have an accurate summary of the two traditions.

It is also safe to say that they are both mistaken. You may want to reply quickly that logically or necessarily it either has to be true that our ordinary concept of freedom is compatible with determinism or that it is not. Just as it either has to be true that you're over six feet tall or that you're not. One or the other has to be true. You may say there is a law of logic about that. But the either-or statement states, or anyway presupposes, something else—that *there is one thing in question with respect to what is called our ordinary idea of freedom.* If there isn't one thing, then saying that our ordinary idea of freedom either is or is not compatible with determinism may be perfectly pointless and in fact as good as false.

In fact, to look back to the first item of our summary of the two traditions, it *is* false to say that everybody shares a single settled concept of freedom. Our reflections on our two attitudes in the last chapter prove that. We can and do think about actions as being free in the sense of being just voluntary, and we also think about actions as being free in the sense of being both voluntary and originated. We do that in real life.

You might ask at this point why, if this is plain, time was taken in the last chapter going through life-hopes, personal feelings, knowledge, moral responsibility, and so on. Part of the answer is that we thereby got a proper idea of the full range of the consequences or implications of determinism. We also got ourselves concentrated on the actuality of the problem. But, you might still ask, couldn't Compatibilism and Incompatibilism have been refuted just by pointing out the fact that we have two ideas of a free choice or action?

I don't think so. By our different method, the method of what you might call recovering our experience, or actually eliciting feelings, we got no less than a proof of the fact that we have the two ideas. It was a proof that is related to something more familiar, a behavioural proof. What one of those comes to, roughly, is establishing that someone has a desire or belief by seeing how he behaves, what he does. Similarly, it is possible to prove that someone has a certain idea by establishing that he has a certain attitude. We found two sets of attitudes, the proof of two ideas.

That is not all. With a certain class of highly relevant persons, including students of philosophy, it very likely would not have been effective just to ask quickly what idea or ideas of a free choice we have, and point out we have two, rather than go through the business of recalling our experience and eliciting feelings. It very likely would not have been effective in the case of anyone familiar with the dispute between Compatibilists and Incompatibilists, and already on a side, maybe very solidly on a side. There would have been the risk of an automatic response to a plain statement of Attitudinism. It is a mortifying fact of life that preconceptions and theories get in the way of seeing facts.

To get back to where we were before that digression, the first and fundamental proposition of both Compatibilists and Incompatibilists is a mistake. We don't have a single settled idea of what has to be true if a choice is to count as free. And our ordinary language doesn't contain such a single idea. The fact of the matter is that 'free' and a lot of related terms are systematically ambiguous. We can use them in the two ways, for voluntary choices and actions, or for both voluntary and originated choices and actions. We don't have *any* definition of a free choice if a definition is supposed to be the one and only correct description of a thing.

To go on to the second part of our summary of the two schools of thought, we already know that each of them has to be wrong in saying that our single idea is whichever they say it is. Returning to the example of the man who behaved badly to my daughter, it is a plain fact that I can think of his choosing to do so just in terms of its being fully voluntary, with what follows from that, and that I can also think of it in terms of its also being a matter of Free Will, with what follows from that.

The third thing said about the two schools of thought was that they agree that we all have a certain necessity-belief, a belief that free choice in one sense is necessary to holding someone responsible or giving him credit for something. This is another mistake. It is a mistake, at any rate, if we understand what seems to be intended, that we all believe a certain statement of fact about one thing's being necessary to another.

That it is a mistake begins to be clear as soon as you ask for the statement of fact. What is it? To take the Compatibilist story, it can't be that just believing a choice was voluntary is *logically* necessary to having a certain attitude to someone—in the way that believing that something is a person is logically necessary to believing that it is a woman. Part of what is involved in holding someone responsible is making a certain evaluation of them, a bad evaluation. But, as moral philosophers have been telling us for a long time, there don't seem to be logical relations of any kind between facts and values, between 'is'-statements and 'ought'-statements.

What is really going on when we think of a choice as having been voluntary is that we are *taking* that as a reason for our feeling about the person, and for actions having to do with him. We *regard* the voluntary choice in a certain way. But to take something as a reason for something else is not to believe that the first thing is logically necessary to the second. If it were, to mention one problem, we could not change our minds about the worth of reasons in the way we do.

I dwell a little bit on this mistake of Compatibilists and Incompatibilists for a certain reason. Their mistake has played a role in making each of their positions a little more persuasive. If we really did have an ordinary belief with a truth value about something's being really necessary to holding people responsible, and no more than that, it would not be likely that we also had a contradictory belief, that something more was necessary. If we really believed it true that only voluntariness in an action was necessary to our having certain feelings about it, we would be unlikely to have the opposite belief that voluntariness was not enough but origination was also required. But there is nothing much surprising in our sometimes taking one thing as a good enough reason for something and our sometimes not doing so—particularly if the thing is somewhat different on different occasions.

Here is a related point. If it really were true that there was some kind of matter of fact, about one thing's being necessary to another, you could expect that we would all agree about it. You could expect that we would all have one idea of a free action in connection with holding people responsible. As some philosophers like to say, there is likely to be convergence in opinion with respect to true propositions. People are likely to come to agree. But the same isn't the case with taking something as a reason for something else. You and I might not agree about whether certain facts are a reason for having an abortion. If the two schools of thought had not made the mistake in question, they would not have been so confident in their views.

The fourth part of our summary of their views was what they had to say about moral responsibility. Compatibilists say determinism leaves it where it is, Incompatibilists say that determinism wrecks it. Both are wrong. Compatibilists are wrong because we know from our reflections that we have one way of holding people responsible, involving an image of origination, that is out of place if determinism is true. Incompatibilists are wrong because we know that we have one way of holding people responsible, involving only an idea of voluntariness, that goes perfectly well with determinism.

To put it differently, Compatibilists go wrong by having some kind of unclear idea of just one of our attitudes, the one involving only voluntariness, and then taking it for the only one we have, and turning it into a single settled definition of free choice and a belief about a necessary relation to something else. Incompatibilists start with some kind of unclear idea of our other attitude, with the origination image in it, and go wrong in the same way. Maybe if either side had seen clearly in connection with moral responsibility that it was just an attitude we have to persons that they were considering, they would not have been so sure that we have only one of them.

While we are on the subject of fundamental disagreement between the two traditions, let me say something else. Each side is confident that it is in possession of the truth. It is a good idea, and often necessary, if you are saying you are in possession of the truth, to have an explanation of why a lot of other people disagree. So each tradition has tried to explain the error of the other. Boiled down, what each explanation comes to is that the other side is just confused or even dim.

Here is a question. Has the problem of the consequences of determinism gone on for centuries because of *confusion?* That is hard to believe. What *would* explain the persistence of the problem is there not being a single settled idea of freedom, but two ideas, involved in different attitudes. What would go further in explaining the persistence of the problem is each of us having the two ideas, and moving back and forth between them. You could say we are at odds with ourselves. So to my mind there is the separate argument for our view that it explains an important part of the history of philosophy.

The fifth and last feature of the two schools of thought is believing that the problem of the consequences of determinism can be settled by logical, intellectual, philosophical, or linguistic means as traditionally conceived. Just look closely at your idea of freedom, get the right definition, check the *Oxford English Dictionary*, and so on. That is one more mistake. The real problem of determinism's consequences is far from being as purely intellectual as the two schools have supposed.

The real problem is that we have got two sets of attitudes, about a lot more than moral responsibility, and this fact issues in our making at least two responses to determinism. To put it differently and a little reductively, we have two sets of desires, and they issue in at least the two responses. That is an uncomfortable situation. But does it amount to a purely intellectual problem, one that we can solve by finding out a truth, or seeing an idea clearly, or showing two propositions to be consistent or inconsistent? I don't think so. For a start, you can't *refute* a desire.

We will go on to the real problem in the next chapter, but first let us get up to date on the persistence of the long battle between Compatibilists and Incompatibilists. It has to be recorded, first, that since the judgements on Compatibilists and Incompatibilists as both wrong was brought to their attention (Honderich 1988), these two parties have not entirely faded away or humbly fallen silent. Not many past members of them have admitted their error and converted to Attitudinism. As already remarked, at least some have gone on proving themselves to be as uniquely in possession of the truth as were Hobbes and Bramhall.

In the last couple of decades, a good deal of diligence has gone into a certain Incompatibilist line of thought laid out by a strong philosopher. Plainly stated, it is that if determinism is true, then my action today, perhaps my going along again with my unjust society, is the effect or consequence of a causal circumstance in the remote past, before I was born. That circumstance, clearly, was not *up to me*. So its necessary consequence, my action of compliance today with my unjust society, is not up to me. Hence my action today is not free and I am not responsible for it. Determinism is inconsistent with freedom and responsibility (van Inwagen).

This line of thought is dignified by having the name of the Consequence Argument for Incompatibilism. It is worth noting in passing that in its essential content, its logic, the argument has nothing to do with our being unable to change the past. It is that the past had in it no act of origination and in particular no relevant act of origination. It had in it no act of origination that had the later action of going along with my unjust society as content or object, so to speak, and as effect. Instead the past had in it that remote causal circumstance and a causal sequence from it leading up to the action of compliance. If the past *did* have such a relevant act of origination in it, although I still couldn't change it or the rest of the past, things would be OK. My action of compliance could be up to me.

It is also worth noting that the argument has nothing essential to do with a causal circumstance *in the remote past*. To repeat, what the Incompatibilist supposes would make my action today up to me, make me free and responsible, is an act of origination relevant to today's action of compliance. Suppose that the act of origination for the action of compliance would have had to be not in the remote past but in the last five minutes—originations wear out, so to speak, if they do not issue in actions within five minutes. If they are to work, they have to be renewed. We do indeed believe something like this. If so, for the Incompatibilist, my action's having been the effect of a causal circumstance just over five minutes ago would make the action not up to me.

Thus what is crucial for this line of thought is a relevant act of origination. And hence, to mention one thing, the argument has as much need of giving an adequate account of origination as any other argument of its ilk—any Incompatibilism. What in fact has happened in connection with the line of argument, however, is a lot of reflection, aided by modal logic, on something else. We could transform it into reflection that makes the essential content or logic of the argument explicit, talk about a causal circumstance just over five minutes ago, but there is no need to do so.

The reflection has been on whether it does really follow, from the fact that a remote causal circumstance was not up to me, that its necessary consequence, my action today, is not up to me. The reflection has included variations on the plain version of the line of thought, and also objections to and supposed refutations of both the plain line of thought and the variations (Ekstrom).

It is not easy for me to see that this has been philosophical time well spent. Does it not seem clear that in an ordinary sense of the words, it does indeed follow that if the remote causal circumstance was not up to me, neither was what was connected with it by an unbroken causal sequence—my action today?

Will anyone say that there is *no* sense of the words in which it follows that if the remote circumstance was not up to me, neither was its necessary consequence? *No* fundamental or important sense in which lack of control is transitive in this way? Might you join me in saying that if modal logic were to prove that there is no such sense of the words, or no important sense of the words, so much the worse for modal logic?

On the other hand, could modal logic or anything else prove that if my action today is the consequence of a certain causal circumstance, there is *no* sense in which it is, say, *up to me*? There is, isn't there, a clear sense in which my action, necessary consequence though it was, may well have been *up to me*—perfectly up to me?

Anyone who still needs persuading might indulge in a little imagining about me. Imagine I was struck a month ago by the philosopher Bradley's utterance that to wish to be better than the world is to be already on the threshold of immorality. Suppose I had then consciously determined after a month's serious reflection that henceforth I would consistently act on the side of my society. Suppose it had come about that a great desire drew me only to this—and of course that I desired to have the desire, and so on. In fact my whole personality and character now supported my action of deference. I could not have been more for it. Does not this conjecture, or any more restrained one you like, clearly establish that it must be a *very* brave Incompatibilist who maintains that there is no significant sense in which my action of compliance was up to me?

Now consider the other side in the traditional dispute—some Compatibilist struggle in the last couple of decades, also deriving from the work of a strong philosopher (Frankfurt). This work mainly centres on a certain kind of example, such as the following one from science fiction.

Polly is faced with a decision between doing the right thing or simply indulging a selfish desire. Polly, being the person she is, decides on the right thing. As a matter of fact, however, even if she had been about to decide to be selfish, she would have decided to do the right thing. This is because there is also a demon neuroscientist in the story. He has implanted a device in her brain such that if she were to be about to decide to do the selfish thing, she would instead decide on the right thing.

What the example shows, it is said, is that a person's moral responsibility with respect to an action doesn't depend on being able to do the other action. It doesn't depend on being able to do otherwise. Polly's being credited with moral responsibility for her action doesn't depend on her having had an alternative.

The example is puzzling, because it is a little vague. You can say, of course, that in a sense Polly *could* have done otherwise—she could have *tried* to decide on or do the selfish thing—and it is for this reason that she gets moral credit for what she did decide. But we do not have to get into that. The example, if it is to be of relevance to us, has to be made entirely definite in a certain way. We have to take the episode as one in which Polly's decision is subject to determinism. It is a decision of which Initiation Determinism, as we called it, was true.

So the example, for all its drama, comes down to the proposition that Polly can be morally responsible, in this case credited with moral responsibility, which presupposes her being free, even if determinism is true. Indeed she can be. And you can explain why. A large part of the explanation is, so to speak, the person Polly is. She is good willed, not seriously selfish. The decision was in accord with her nature. Also, she was in no sense constrained or compelled to make the decision—it was not against any serious desire or impulse of hers. In short, the decision was voluntary.

But now what has been proved? Well, I guess it has been proved, if a little proof will do, that we have an idea of freedom that is consistent with determinism. But we are supposed to have a proof of Compatibilism. *That* doctrine has been to the effect that our *single* idea of freedom, or single important one, is the idea of voluntariness. Has this been proved? Obviously not. In fact there is no difficulty at all in presenting and colouring examples so as to prove the existence of the idea of freedom that includes origination. Indeed this could be done with the example of Polly. It can be presented as an instance of a completely determined decision and hence as one in which a decision in a certain sense is unfree. I contentedly leave that to you.

Let me mention yet more quickly some more industry by Compatibilists, owed to an idea of the same philosopher (Frankfurt; cf. Dennett; Lehrer; Magill). It might be taken as at bottom the effort to show why kleptomaniacs, compulsive hand-washers, and other such unfortunates, often taken as unfree in their behaviour, are also such on the Compatibilist account of freedom. Certainly, it can be thought there is a problem for the account here, since the kleptomaniac in walking out of the department store yet again without paying for the blouses presumably *is* somehow doing what he wants to do, presumably is *not* acting against desire.

Compatibilists are indeed on the way to a solution if they suppose, a little bravely, that all kleptomaniacs not only desire to make off with the blouses, but also desire *not* to have that desire. By means of this idea of a hierarchy of desires, that is, the Compatibilist is indeed improving his conception of a free action—it is, at least in the first part of the conception, an action such that we desire to desire to perform it. Suppose more than that—that the whole philosophical enterprise, this hierarchical theory of freedom, works like a dream, with no difficulties about a regress or about identifying a self with a particular level of desires or about anything else.

Will that have come near to establishing that there is no other conception of a free action? Will it come close to establishing that we have operating in our lives only the hierarchic conception? Will it come close to establishing the lesser thing, to which some Compatibilists have recently tended to retreat, that this conception is fundamental or dominant or most salient or in some other way ahead of another one? Come to think of it, *how* could it actually do that? Are we to suppose that from the premise that one conception of freedom has now been really perfected it follows that there is no other conception of freedom or none worth attention?

So it is hard for me to agree that the Incompatibilist and Compatibilist regiments should have gone on proving that one of them has the truth. What each of them has actually been doing for the most part, and it has been work of value, is to clarify and develop their particular conceptions of freedom—improve further on successors to Bramhall's idea of origination and Hobbes's idea of voluntariness. They have not seen themselves and their humbler project aright. If they have served a philosophical purpose, it is still satisfactory to record that the two regiments are no longer alone in the field, as we shall see in due course (pp. 142–3). It is also satisfactory that there have been famous defections from their ranks, or anyway uncertainty as to whether certain captains are still with them.

Professor Kane, who sometimes still seems to be at the head of the Free Will regiment, can nevertheless now write that 'freedom' definitely *can* mean something compatible with determinism. He can add that

I think those of us who believe in a free will that is incompatible with determinism—we Incompatibilists and libertarians so-called—should simply concede this point to our Compatibilist opponents. Many kinds of freedom worth wanting are indeed compatible with determinism. What we Incompatibilists should be insisting upon instead is that there is *at least one* kind of freedom worth wanting that is incompatible with determinism. (Kane 2002c; cf. 2002d)

It is unclear in what sense this is Incompatibilism, certainly, since it allows that we are concerned with the other kind of freedom.

As indicated, Incompatibilism may be in process of reducing itself to the claim that its idea of freedom is *more important to us* than the other one. Maybe that we *want it more*. Can it really be that the brave battle between Incompatibilists and Compatibilists, from Hobbes and Bramhall onwards, about the factual question of whether freedom is compatible with determinism, about our supposed single and settled concept of freedom, is to come down in the end to a little quarrel about which of two kinds of freedom would be better for us, maybe do more for our dignity?

That would be sad for traditionalists, but in fact an improvement on the old stuff. That is not to say that Incompatibilists would be right, that they could actually defend their new position. It is far from an evident truth. Compatibilists would have several replies. Take moral and legal rights, whole structures of them, so important in our societies and in relations between them. They have to do with freedom, obviously, and perhaps nothing about freedom gets more attention. It is clear that the rights ordinarily have to do only with ensuring the voluntariness of actions by individuals. What bills of rights seek to do is preserve us from certain constraints and compulsions.

So there is a good reply for Compatibilists. But as in the case of the dispute between the two parties until recently, the factual dispute supposedly about a single concept of freedom, what needs to be said about an essentially evaluative dispute is that neither party wins. We do give importance, in different contexts, to the two ideas of freedom.

There is also Professor Fischer, also prominent in this part of philosophy. He is, as he says, a Semi-Compatibilist. Determinism in his view is incompatible with freedom, but compatible with moral responsibility. This seems rather more than a fracture in the iceberg of Compatibilism. Certainly, it is not hard to agree that there is *a* conception of freedom incompatible with determinism, and *a* conception of moral responsibility that is compatible with it. This follows from there being two conceptions or versions of each of these things. Should Professor Fischer not give up his old allegiance completely and join the the Attitudinists?

The real problem raised by determinism, to go back to it, is that

COMPATIBILISM AND INCOMPATIBILISM 121

each of us has the two ideas of freedom contained in two families of attitudes, each fundamental, and this results in two responses to determinism and an uncomfortable situation. Let us go on to this real problem.

10

AFFIRMATION

THE real problem of determinism and freedom is at bottom the finding or making of a *satisfactory* response to the likely truth of determinism. That is the problem we face now. Our enquiry first into the conceptual adequacy of a theory of determinism, then into the evidence for it, and then into what has been considered so far of its consequences in terms of two sets of attitudes and two responses—all of that enquiry culminates in this problem. We have more on our plate than, say, the little puzzle of whether 'He could have done better by her', in its one and only correct usage, means something consistent with his choices and actions being effects. It is in fact a spurious puzzle, because there isn't any such thing as the one and only correct usage. But leave all that.

Our situation is that we have the two sets of attitudes, both including life-hopes, personal feelings, attitudes about knowledge, and various moral feelings. One set involves images of origination or Free Will with respect to actions, and the other does not. This is what we are calling Attitudinism. With the first set of attitudes, if we bring it together with the truth of determinism, or of course near-determinism (p. 5), our response may be dismay. We may feel the attitudes must be abandoned because they are inconsistent with determinism. With the second family, our response can be intransigence. We will soldier on, whatever else is true. These attitudes can go together with determinism.

That situation is unsatisfactory. What we need to try to do is to take into account all of it, and find or make a new response to determinism. We need to get into a different way of feeling about determinism. We need to come to a response that takes into account not only its truth, and the two sets of attitudes, but also the two responses we may have in the first instance, dismay and intransigence. So the final upshot, if we are successful, will partly be a response to the two initial responses.

The unsatisfactoriness of the situation we are in, to have it clear, is a matter of several things. For a start, dismay is rightly named. It can be no joy to us. Having a kind of hopes dashed, a kind of personal feelings obstructed, a grip on reality put in doubt, a way of moral disapproval undercut, a kind of self-estimation denied to us—none of this is tolerable. Nor is something else tolerable. We *act* on some of the feelings in question, notably moral disapproval. We do things to people. Not much has been said of these actions so far, and the subject will get separate consideration in the next chapter. But obviously this fact must make for a particular kind of consternation. Have we been and are we now involved in systematic unkindness and injustice, not only personally but as members of a society?

If dismay is unsatisfactory, so is intransigence. There is not much to be said for it. Certainly we can fix our attention on the family of attitudes consistent with determinism, and try to plough on ahead. But as you will have thought, there is an element of bluff in this, and we can't persist in it. We can't actually hypnotize ourselves into forgetting that we have those other attitudes, that other family, and that they don't go with determinism. When I think about my future just in terms of my true nature being expressed and my desires not being defeated, something else will be in a corner of my mind, the thought that if determinism is true, my future is fixed.

Might it be, by the way, that this attitude of Intransigence is a little less sustainable, or more unsustainable, than has so far been suggested? Have I perhaps taken it to be more durable than it really is—because I have supposed that there must be some considerable source or impulse which lies behind the Compatibilist tradition, the official acceptance of freedom as only voluntariness? Well, intransigence does seem to be a part of ordinary life. For a start, we can certainly be impatient with anybody who offers determinism as a defence for themselves. We are apt to maintain that the strong attitudes in which we want to persist are consistent with it and all that matters.

Does our situation involve a third unsatisfactoriness, that we are trapped in inconsistency? This is a little complicated.

Certainly it is not only propositions or statements, things that are true or false in the fundamental sense, that can be inconsistent. We can in some way give inconsistent orders, and be subject to inconsistent desires. To want to be with someone, and also want not to be with them, is inconsistent. That is near to saying what is certainly the case, that we can have inconsistent attitudes. But consider in particular being morally disapproving of someone, in the way that involves thinking of the action as voluntary, and not being morally disapproving of them in the way that involves picturing the action as also originated. Is there inconsistency in this case? In fact there isn't, since what one *is* doing is not the same thing as the thing one *isn't* doing. They are different kinds of moral disapproval. The situation is the same when we have one kind of hope for our future and do not have the other kind—the one involving origination. If the various pairs of attitudes we have been thinking about *were* inconsistent, by the way, that would be a reason for doubting that each of us has both of them.

There isn't inconsistency to be found, either, by way of a nearby idea. It is that we take the freedom of an action to consist in voluntariness plus origination, and also take it to consist in just voluntariness. In fact we don't do both. We may first suppose one and then later the other, but that does not make us inconsistent. Inconsistency of the standard sort is something like believing conflicting things at the same time.

To leave the attitudes, is there inconsistency in the two responses of dismay and intransigence? Dismay about life-hopes is the response that our hopes are destroyed by determinism, and intransigence is the response that they are untouched by it. Again it is possible to say that we cannot be charged with inconsistency because we do not make the two responses together. Still, it is true that we may well find ourselves pulled in both directions. If that is so, we are certainly on the way to inconsistency if not in it. We are close to having inconsistent desires.

The feeling that our situation as described does involve real inconsistency is very likely mainly owed to something else which is certainly related. There is another discomfort, already noticed. Our situation in its very essence includes instability or oscillation, moving back and forth between two positions. It is not as if we can without further ado and by an act of will commit ourselves once and for all to one family of attitudes. Suppose I try just to plump for intransigence about my feelings of moral disapproval. Henceforth, I tell myself, I will not have retributive feelings or act on them. That is easier said than done. I know this if I think of a real hurt done to myself or someone close to me.

Given the unsatisfactoriness of our situation, we need to do something. What are we to do? In general terms, the answer is clear. If we think determinism or near-determinism is true, what we have to do is try to give up whatever depends on thoughts inconsistent with it. Above all we have to try to accept the defeat of certain desires. This is bound up with trying to be happier about, or more reconciled to, the desires in which we can persist, the ones consistent with determinism. We can try to do this by various particular means. I do not suggest exactly that we should set out to manipulate our feelings, but that we may be able to reflect on them to some effect.

That proposal may be less than clear, unclear in its relation to our line of reflection so far and the categories we have been using. Indeed, as so often happens, useful categories can come to obscure things.

To put the proposal differently, what we need to see first is that our attitudes involving voluntariness cannot really allow us to be intransigent, to go on as if determinism changes nothing. We can't successfully barricade ourselves in them. And secondly, our attitudes involving both voluntariness and origination need not give rise to dismay, taking everything as wrecked. That is to forget that in part or in a way these attitudes can persist. They can persist in so far as they involve voluntariness. What that comes to, as you will guess, is that they can persist *in so far* as they are identical with the attitudes involving voluntariness.

A last comparison with Compatibilism and Incompatibilism will also be useful, although no doubt you can work it out for yourself. What is being proposed differs from both of those traditions in that it fully recognizes the existence of two kinds of attitudes involving different conceptions—where Compatibilism and Incompatibilism claim we have a single settled belief. What is being proposed has to do with one kind of attitudes, involving only voluntariness, which kind is of course related to the single belief assigned to us by Compatibilism. But what is being proposed *also* has to do with the other attitudes, with origination in them, related to the single belief bestowed on us by Incompatibilism. The proposal is not much more like Compatibilism than Incompatibilism.

To put the proposal in a nutshell, our new response should be this: trying *by various strategies* to *accommodate ourselves to the situation we find ourselves in—accommodate ourselves to just what we can really possess if determinism is true, accommodate ourselves to the part of our lives that does not rest on the illusion of Free Will.* We can reflect on what is perhaps the limited worth of what we have to give up, consider possible compensations of a belief in determinism, take care not to underestimate what we can have, and consider a certain prospect having to do with genuine and settled belief in determinism.

To try to make this response, which can be called *affirmation*, is to try to change our feeling about a part of life or our outlook on a part of life. Indeed, to try to make the response of affirmation is to try to arrive at one part of what is rightly called a philosophy of life. The kind of thing I mean is not an answer to the question of the meaning of life, whatever that question may be. Certainly, a philosophy of life in my sense does not have to do with a deep purpose or goal of our existence. It may have nothing to do with religion. Rather, a philosophy of life consists in feelings in which we can persist, feelings that give us some support and which are as satisfactory as truth will allow. Some of them, the ones relevant to our present concern, will be acceptings or rejectings of certain possible attitudes and things, those we have been thinking about.

It is certainly true that contemporary philosophers, at any rate philosophers within the English language, are inclined to recoil from philosophies of life. Their understandable reason for this is that most philosophies of life even of the defined kind do not measure up to certain intellectual and philosophical standards. But maybe the standards are the wrong ones. It needs to be remembered that some of the greatest of philosophers have attempted to arrive at such outlooks. Plato, Aristotle, Spinoza, Kant, Russell, and Wittgenstein, if he is to be included in the list, have in very different ways recommended philosophies of life. None of that matters too much. What does matter is that the only possible solution to the problem of determinism is the sort of thing that can be regarded as part of such a philosophy. If we recoil from it, we recoil from the chance of a solution.

What has been said so far about the accommodation we need to make has been very general. Let us now look a bit more closely at possible means of getting into a satisfactory state about determinism.

Is there help in the thought that what we need to give up does not come to much? I have in mind something that became clear when we were looking at the philosophy of mind and action in terms of Free Will or origination. For all their struggles, the Free Will philosophers have never given much content to the central ideas on which they depend. Their talk of the self or an originator is talk of nothing very clear. Talk of the activity of origination, which is supposed to help, has not got much content (see pp. 46ff., 50).

Perhaps it is near to true that the philosophical struggles have not made much advance on what we have been calling our ordinary image of origination. What we have is just a kind of notion of choices coming about in such a way that they are not a matter of cause and effect but we are in a certain way responsible for them. They come about in such a way that we can be held responsible for them, get moral credit for them, and persist in various other attitudes in a way that is impossible if determinism is true.

It seems to me that we will not get very far in our programme of renunciation by this means. One reason is the general truth that feelings do not depend on having clear and worked-out contents. The contents do not have to satisfy an analytic philosopher. They do not wane or evaporate because they do not measure up in this way. Indeed, some of them depend on and persist because of their vagueness. We do have what may be somewhat over-described as nameless fears. A lot of less dramatic feelings are by their nature not explicit.

There is a larger reason why this slightly too intellectual strategy is unlikely to work. What we are being invited to eschew, however conceptually thin, is exactly what attracts us. Exactly what raises my hopes, my hopes of the kind inconsistent with determinism, is the promise of my somehow overcoming things as they are and will be, my not being bound by causation. But that *is* the image of origination.

A very different idea about how we might move towards affirmation has to do with nature, by which I mean the nonhuman world. There has been a long history of thought and feeling which has to do in a certain way with our relation to nature. In part, this has involved the recommendation that we somehow get into connection with it, somehow identify or associate ourselves with it, or at least be guided by it. The idea is that there is a great reward in this.

Early Greek philosophers and many other people since have advocated that we live our lives in harmony with nature. Often enough this kind of advocacy has involved a somehow spiritualized conception of nature. The philosopher Spinoza provides an example. What exists, for him, is the single thing which can be called God or Nature. By entering into a certain relation to it, we can achieve peace of mind, perhaps what he famously called 'the intellectual love of God'. Others have said I can escape the triviality of my individual existence, and also try to deal with the prospect of my death, by identifying with something greater. The literature of Romanticism, above all the poetry, has in it a different but related impulse. Marx and Engels in yet other ways recommend a kind of acceptance of nature. Engels speaks of a tranquillity to be had from accepting nature as determined. He is a long way from a contemporary philosopher who still refers to determinism as 'the hideous hypothesis' (Hampshire).

Can we in this way see a certain compensation in determinism, and thus an incentive to accepting what it entails? There is certainly a particular sense in which determinism enables us to identify with nature, or, as might even be said, to regard ourselves as having membership in nature. This is so since determinism is unique in asserting that we stand in a close and unproblematic connection with nature. It is a long way from Romantic poetry. In terms of the theory of determinism we have been considering, this closeness is a matter both of the mind–brain relation and of the causation of all of our mental existence. We are not detached from nature, but more or less in it.

To take up a view that puts us in a close and unproblematic connection with nature might be thought to make it easier to enter into the ways of feeling recommended to us. Determinism, it might be supposed, is indeed a way to tranquillity. It offers this reward for self-denial in terms of attitudes that we are attempting.

It is not easy to say very much about this. One thing that stands in the way is the feeling that anything said will be merely personal, not of any general import. But I find it hard to resist the feeling that most of us are unlikely to get far forward by this means in giving up what we need to give up if determinism is true. Certainly, not many of us in this twenty-first century can share in the inclination to ascribe a spiritual character to nature. Also, we are not one with the young Shelley, who in *Queen Mab* managed to write a paean of praise to determinism itself.

There is something else very different that is more promising. In connection with our personal feelings, which are not moral feelings, it was mentioned that some of them are directed to ourselves. Some of them are against ourselves. Also, of course, I can morally approve and disapprove of myself. So—I may have kinds of non-moral disdain for myself and I may hold myself morally responsible. I do in both these ways regard myself as a failure. Sometimes what I have failed in is no small thing. I can feel that I have failed to do what would have realized a great hope. Perhaps I have failed to find something out. I can feel that I have failed in my life.

Feelings of failure have to do with my actions, actions initiated by me. According to the general view we have, these feelings are of two kinds. In the one case, they are feelings that involve my contemplating the action as owed to me in the sense that it was voluntary. It was my action in that it came from me and my desires and so on. The other kind of feeling of failure involves my seeing the action as owed to me in the stronger sense that it was also originated by me. I take it as mine in a stronger sense.

It is feelings of failure of the second sort that are sharper. It is here that the grim verdict that *I* have failed seems most in place. There was something within my grasp, something that I had a chance to do or not do, and *I* did not measure up. If we really take determinism to be true, we can rightly seek to escape from these darkest feelings. Determinism offers the compensation of an escape from a mordant kind of self-dislike and self-disapproval. Whatever is to be said in the end about the enterprise of accommodating ourselves to determinism, we here have something more promising than the thinness of our thoughts about origination or anything about being one with nature.

You may be quick to add that something else must go with this renunciation of failure, and of course you are right. There is a kind of success or credit I cannot have if determinism is true. Still, might it be that eschewing both the failure and the success is a good bargain? It is possible to feel this.

In trying to get a fuller picture of the response of affirmation, further things can be said about each of the parts of life which we know to be affected by determinism. With respect to life-hopes, it needs to be kept in mind that those that are consistent with determinism can in a sense be as unbounded or unlimited as those that we need to give up. Take what can be called objects of hope (pp. 91–2). Any object of a hope of the second kind can also be an object of a hope of the first kind. However grand or private or idiosyncratic a state of affairs I have in mind, I can go on hoping for it in the only way that remains possible to me.

It is also worth keeping in mind something about the intrinsic nature of good hopes, the difference between them and the conceivable circumstance of now being *certain* about some future state of affairs. It is possible to think that a life of *certainties* about the future, however satisfactory those certainties, would be less attractive than a life of good hopes realized. This particular attractiveness does not disappear if we are restricted to hopes that are consistent with determinism. Taking determinism to be true, as we know, is far from taking the future to be predictable by us. To make use of Spinoza's definition of hope, our lives can still have in them unsteady joy with respect to an issue about which we are in doubt.

Consider personal feelings about others for a moment. We have the prospect of withdrawing from the negative or resentful ones which have a special quality owed to our image of origination, the idea that those who disregard or injure us really could have done better by us. To think of our actions in reply, we also have the prospect of escaping the self-accusation which must come from persisting in what is made irrational by determinism. We can think too of the positive or appreciative personal feelings about others in which we can persist. We do not have to do anything like *give up* gratitude. We do not have to take as weak or unsatisfactory the kind of gratitude in which we can persist. If I think of my sister's tender gift to me, this is no insignificant feeling because it focuses not on an image of origination but rather on ideas of her feelings for me. So with my response to good judgements on me. I am not going to be left without the possibility of taking pleasure in whatever admiration others have for me. The world need not go cold.

As for knowledge, here as everywhere something must go. We cannot persist in a certain confidence or aspiration about reality. Our situation is something like the one to which we are assigned by a considerable number of metaphysical philosophers, notably

Plato. They speak of a reality beyond, something out of reach. But allowing that determinism affects us in the given way, and restricts us to certain paths of enquiry, is far from allowing that it consigns us to a discontented ignorance or agnosticism. We keep that knowledge that is the great product of our uncoerced desire to know.

The general idea will now be clear. With respect to each of the parts of our lives affected by determinism, we must accept certain things, but we can find facts of a reassuring kind. It is true that where we find actual gains, losses seem to go with them. We cannot escape a kind of hatred and keep the counterpart kind of love. But with respect to that point, is there *any* possibility of our changing so that we escape the hatred and keep some variant of the counterpart love? It may be worth thinking about.

What it all comes to, as perhaps a critic would say, is looking on the bright side, or putting a good face on things, or even making the best of a bad job. That is a bit unkind and perhaps not serious enough, but not far off the truth. What is more important is a large question. Can we succeed? In fact, it is hard to be confident. We can go some way forward, but it is possible to think that none of the assuagements and solaces will enable us really to succeed in the response of affirmation. It would be a response, by the way, that can have more to it than simply the giving-up of some things and the valuing of others. It would be central to a celebratory philosophy of life. That is something far from resignation or defeat.

But let us stick to the question. If it is hard to be confident of achieving affirmation in the ways we have looked at, is there any more to be said? There are two things.

We, or at any rate very nearly all of us, do not believe in determinism. It goes against the great tradition of our culture. We are prisoners of that culture, bound by inherited ways of feeling. Some of us are in some real sense persuaded by what is said for determinism and yet do not believe. There is a paradox there, but also a truth. I have no doubt that it is possible to agree with the arguments of this book and yet to be hesitant. Anyone in such a position has one more strategy—to try really to believe what he or she takes to be at least the truer view.

The last and connected thing is simply that *true belief* in determinism, as against assuagements and solaces, is the only thing that will enable us really to succeed in the response of affirmation.

Nothing else can be certain. Whatever is said of wishing, we do not go on fully desiring what we *really believe* we cannot have. We do not spend time on it. We, or those who come after us, will not desire what they really believe is not to be had. They will have no need to give up in life either.

11

PUNISHMENT, SOCIETY, POLITICS

W E now have a solution, I think *the* solution, to the problem of the consequences of determinism. That the solution is new may in itself be an argument for it. If either of Compatibilism or Incompatibilism were actually *true*, wouldn't its proponents have succeeded by now in getting agreement on the fact? They've worked hard enough, and been at it for at least a couple of centuries. As for our own line of thought, there are some large facts that have so far been put to one side. We need to see how they are affected by our solution to the problem of the consequences of determinism.

We have been asking how determinism or near-determinism affects us in our more or less private lives, and what we need to try to do as a result. This is not just a matter of our attitudes or feelings, of course. As remarked in passing earlier, we act on our attitudes, affecting other people. We may act differently according to whether in our personal and moral feelings we take it that what someone said or did was just voluntary or was also a matter of Free Will. The solution we have to the problem of the consequences of determinism needs to be extended to what can be described as actions of society, and are usually called social institutions, practices, and the like. Certainly, determinism affects them.

So far we have managed to keep moral and political and any other evaluative kinds of philosophy out of our deliberations. We have not been concerned with anything like Jeremy Bentham's Principle of Utility or Greatest Happiness Principle, that we ought always to do the action which will produce the greatest total of happiness, or the different idea that we should always act in such a way that people get their just deserts. We *might* have considered consequences of determinism for these moral principles or outlooks when we were looking at our moral feelings, but it was simpler not to do so. There was also the good reason that these consequences are better considered in connection with our present and last subject, which is social institutions and the like.

In fact, moral principles cannot be kept out of this subject. This is so for the reason that it would be hopeless to ask about the consequences of determinism for, say, punishment generally. There are different possible kinds of punishment, which is to say kinds of punishment owed to different moral principles and different combinations of these. Determinism affects these kinds of punishment differently. The same is true with all of our social facts. It is punishment we shall actually consider, while keeping in mind the others.

The second of these social facts is a society's rewarding of people who do not break its laws. Law-abiders, at least if they are ordinarily lucky, are left to live their lives without the interference of the criminal courts and the prisons. The third social fact is a society's way of distributing greater or lesser incomes to its members, and the fourth its way of distributing wealth and other property. No doubt it would be mistaken to think that every society has what would ordinarily be called a central agency of distribution for these things. But that is not of much importance. Every society and in particular every government does at least support a particular distribution, however the distribution may have come about.

The fifth social fact is that of positions of relative power, and the sixth is positions of rank, authority, standing, and the like. The two are connected but distinguishable. To take one example, it is possible to have authority without power, at least for a while. The seventh fact is praise and blame, or commendation and condemnation. These fall short of being reward and punishment, and need to be separated from what we have already considered, moral approval and moral disapproval. I can approve or disapprove of someone without saying so, and indeed without performing any noticeable action. In all societies there is a lot of praising and blaming, usually by persons in positions of power or authority.

The moral outlooks with respect to punishment have long been called theories of the justification of punishment. They are called theories, no doubt, because they offer explanations of what people have taken to be a fact—the fact that punishment by the state or some states *is* right or morally justified. But it is more than a little presumptuous to assume that all state punishment, or even most state punishment, is in fact right. Most of us can think of particular states which seem to falsify the generalization. Let us use the description 'theory of punishment' in a loose way, however, to mean an attempt to justify punishment or show it is right.

Each of these theories faces a number of questions. The first one is what the theory comes to. As in the case of any theory of determinism or of origination, it is all too possible that what is on offer is not clear, consistent, and worked-out. The second question is whether the theory really does give us at least a prima facie argument for punishment.

If a theory doesn't pass those two tests, we needn't spend time on it. If it does, we can then consider it with respect to our main subject. Is the theory affected by determinism? More important, is the possible or actual system of punishment which the theory supports affected by determinism? That comes down to the question of whether the system involves the assumption that the actions of offenders are originated. If so, what possibility is there of making the response of affirmation in connection with it?

A last question, which will not concern us much, has to do with the fact that what we are calling theories of punishment are often combined into a package. These days most of these theories come in packages—called theories themselves, of course (Duff; Lacey). The last question is whether a particular theory, affected or not by determinism, matters very much to the package it is in.

One theory that may come to mind in connection with determinism, although not first of all, is that offenders somehow freely *agree* to their punishments. It has recently had a popularity owed to the unpopularity of what is called the prevention theory. The latter, sometimes associated with Bentham's Greatest Happiness Principle, is of course that punishment is justified because it prevents offences. It reduces the number of offences in the future. In good part, this is the idea that A must go to prison in order to stop B and C from breaking the law. That has the flavour of making use of A, and the flavour is unpopular. Suppose it can be shown that A has actually freely agreed to go to prison. Then in sending him there we will also be paying attention to *him*, not just regarding him as a means to a general end.

One version of the agreement theory begins from a clear idea (Nino). What it is for me to agree or consent to a thing is just to do some act of which I know the thing to be a necessary consequence. This definition of agreement is upsetting to some people in some connections, but there is an argument that it defines agreement as that is understood in the civil as against the criminal law. Certainly there is no objection on the ground that agreement of this kind does not involve a document or a verbal promise. *Any* definition of agreement has to cover putting up one's hand at the auction.

The heart of this version of the agreement theory is that an offender when he offends is performing an act of which he knows something to be a necessary consequence. It cannot reasonably be said, of course, that that thing is his being punished. He certainly does not regard that as a necessary consequence. The necessary consequence is said to be his loss of his immunity to punishment. He knows that by offending he becomes what he was not before, a candidate for punishment.

The theory in this form is a lot better than in other obscure forms that preceded it and indeed have followed it, but let me mention one reaction to it. It is that if our intention is really to pay attention to the offender, and not just to use him as a means to a general end, we are not doing much of a job of it. If *he* is to be shown a kind of personal respect, there is something that might be thought more important than that he has in a sense consented to his loss of immunity to punishment. It is that he strenuously does not consent in any sense to his punishment, as he will show by his other actions, such as avoiding policemen.

To my mind, what we have here is an example of a theory of punishment that does not pass the initial test of providing us with a prima facie argument for punishment. Since life is short, we need not press on to ask about the bearing of determinism on it. I suspect that the upshot would be that the kind of free act the theory requires on the part of the offender, although proponents of the theory may have had origination in mind, could be no more than voluntariness. That is, there would be the possibility of the response of affirmation in connection with the theory.

As it seems to me, the story is the same with other agreement theories of punishment. One is contained in the very impressive political philosophy of John Rawls. This theory supposes that each offender in his true nature, a kind of rational or moral nature, sees that punishment is right in certain circumstances. So he can be said to agree to his own punishment. One great difficulty about this is that it is individuals, not parts of individuals, however respectable those parts, that make agreements. It certainly doesn't follow from the fact that I felt a moral obligation to buy something from you that *I* agreed to buy it.

The theory of punishment that is likely to come to mind first in connection with determinism is that punishment is right because it is *deserved*. This is the retribution theory. What we really have here is again a number of versions or forms of a theory. This is so for the reason that different meanings are assigned to claims that someone deserves something for something else. There has never been agreement on what these desert-claims are to be taken as meaning.

People sometimes speak as if a deserved penalty just *is* a penalty that is right. If we take them seriously, and try to use that idea in a retribution theory, we get a useless circularity. The theory is that imposing a penalty on someone is right because it is the deserved penalty. But what that comes to, on the given understanding, is that the penalty is right because it is right. A better idea, but not a good one, is that a penalty's being deserved is its being equivalent to the offence. That is, there is some *fact* of equivalence between the distress of the penalty and the culpability of the offender. Judges often seem to have this idea in mind, and seem not to see its problems.

One of these problems is that it is pretty hard to find the fact in question. It is unclear how we are to quantify or measure the penalty. And can we put numbers on culpability at all? Above all, it seems inconceivable that we should be able to quantify both the penalty and the culpability in the same units. If that is so, and they are not commensurable, how can there ever be a fact that a distress is or is not equivalent to a culpability?

Perhaps we can find a different kind of fact. It has been suggested that a certain penalty is in fact equivalent to an offence in a somewhat surprising way. Ordinary persons would be indifferent if they had to choose between suffering the penalty and having the offence committed against them. If they had to choose, they wouldn't care which. Whatever else is to be said about this, it seems to be open to a considerable objection. Suppose that we have an offender and we are totally confident that in the indirect way a certain penalty is equivalent to his offence. Why is this fact a reason, a moral reason, for imposing the penalty on him? When we remember that there are endless pairs of equivalent things in this sense, having nothing to do with penalties and offences, it seems that the fact is not a moral reason for action at all.

Yet another retribution theory starts by talking not of a penalty itself, but of the suffering or frustration it involves. In answer to the question of what it means to say that a certain suffering is deserved by a guilty man, what we are told is just that it is intrinsically good that the guilty suffer (L. H. Davies). This theory may bring to mind the very first one at which we glanced, but it avoids the circularity. What this theory comes to is the uncircular argument that imposing a particular *penalty* on somebody is right because the *suffering* of the guilty is an intrinsic good.

There are at least two objections to this view. One is that what we expect to get in a retribution theory is some kind of fact to support the conclusion that it is right to punish. Other retribution theories try to provide a fact. What we get in this one is not a fact to start off with, but nothing other than a moral judgement, as disputable as any other moral judgement. The other objection has to do with that moral judgement. Anybody, it seems, can announce that something is an intrinsic good. I can now say that it is an intrinsic good that the guilty should be reformed, or better that the only intrinsic good is the prevention of suffering.

We have not got to a retribution theory that passes the first tests mentioned in the beginning. We have not got to one that is conceptually adequate and that also gives a prima facie reason for punishment. It seems to me that there must be such a theory, whatever is to be said of it in the end. There must be *something* substantial in talk of desert and punishment.

Suppose we think of real life. Think of somebody's being vilified, robbed of their means of life, cheated in some financial arrangement, lied about by a policeman, molested, raped, maimed, or killed. Suppose someone says the offender should get what he deserves. The same thing may be said in many other ways. The offender should get his just or rightful deserts. The law should take its course. He shouldn't get away with it, or should pay his debt. He should get what is owing to him, or what is coming to him. The victim or those related to the victim should get satisfaction.

What cannot be avoided, like it or not, is the thought that there is a real argument in this sort of thing. It is that punishing the offender will give satisfaction to the victim or others, perhaps to society as a whole. The offender by his offence has created a grievance, by which I mean a desire on the part of other people for exactly his distress. Punishing him will satisfy that desire. Further, there is one particular penalty that in a clear sense will be equivalent to his offence. That is the penalty that does not do more and does not do less than exactly satisfy the grievance.

This is not a new idea but it is not popular. Philosophers and others attracted to retribution have put a lot of energy into trying to prove that there is a retribution theory a lot better than this, with better moral tone. I don't think myself that they have succeeded. What they always produce is something like the weak theories at which we have glanced. There must be some clear prima facie reason for punishment in talk of desert over centuries, and in this theory we have such a reason. That it seems distasteful does not make it not a reason.

At last we do have something, a possible kind of punishment, about which we can raise the issue of determinism. What is needed for this kind of punishment is an action that gives rise to grievance, to desires for the distress of the offender. It is clear that what is needed is a free action, but what sort? Is just a voluntary action required, or an action that is also taken as originated? If determinism is taken as true, what is its upshot for the kind of punishment in question and the theory that justifies it?

The answer goes together with and indeed follows from a conclusion at an earlier stage of our enquiry. When we were first looking at the responses of dismay and intransigence, we distinguished a kind of moral disapproval, a way of holding other people responsible. We took it that this kind of feeling, owed to someone else's injuring us, includes what were called our retributive desires—and that they are dependent on taking the other person's action as not only voluntary but also originated (pp. 101–2). The very same things might have been said about one kind of personal feelings, one kind of resentful feelings.

The desires involved in these kinds of moral and personal feelings are of the same category as those involved in retributive punishment as we are now understanding it. All of these desires are vulnerable to belief in determinism. They cannot persist. At long last we then have our first conclusion about determinism and punishment. If determinism is true and *if*—it is a big if—there is any institution of punishment whose only recommendation is that it is retributive in the way we have in mind, that institution should be abandoned. Those who support it need to make a certain response to their situation. That response should be affirmation. A part of it will indeed be giving up their institution of punishment.

That is not the end of this part of the story. You may agree that anyone in the position we are contemplating will in fact have another reason for giving up the punishment in question. It is wrong or unjustified. The theory which supports it is intolerable. It cannot be that we should satisfy grievance by imposing great distress on other people. The means of great distress is not justified by the end of satisfaction.

Another thing is a lot more important. It was said earlier that theories of punishment are nowadays put into packages or larger theories. The retribution theory as we have it, I hope, is no longer held on its own by anyone. There are, I hope, no institutions of punishment whose intention is just to satisfy grievance. It is hard to think that an institution of punishment could in fact have only this to be said for it. But some retribution theory or other *is* taken by many people to be part of a package-theory that does justify punishment. Actual institutions of punishment *are* run partly in accordance with a retribution theory. It seems to me that the retribution theory in question has to be the unpalatable one that has been explained.

You will not need to have the further conclusion spelled out. It is that if determinism is true, it affects these package-theories and these institutions. The theories have to be abandoned in part, and the institutions have to be at least changed.

The most common sort of package-theory is to the effect that punishment is justified because it is *both* preventive and deserved. This sort of theory does in fact issue in actual institutions of punishment. They are the institutions of punishment in the societies of which we know. They are partly run in accordance with the retribution idea. A prisoner's sentence may be prolonged not for a preventive reason but for the retributive reason. If determinism is true, the package-theories have in part got to be abandoned. The institutions need to be changed. Making those changes will be part of the response of affirmation.

The response of affirmation does not limit us to only one theory and practice of punishment. Another possibility is Bentham's Utilitarian theory: punishment is right when it prevents offences and in so doing produces the greatest total of happiness. It seems to me, however, that there is a better one. It is that punishment is right when it is fair, when it has fair consequences. That is, it is right when it is in accordance with a certain moral principle. That principle is the Principle of Equality, which is that we should take really effective steps to make well-off those who are badly-off (Honderich 1981). Our societies should be on that path, and should have the institutions of punishment that help.

Philosophers concerned with the problem of the consequences of determinism have usually given some attention to punishment. They have not attended to other social facts. But, as remarked in the beginning, determinism does have consequences for more social facts than punishment. It has consequences for what we can as well call the social actions that enter into the rewarding of law-abiders, distributions of income and of wealth, distributions of power and rank, and official praising and blaming.

What is true of punishment is true to a greater or lesser extent with these other institutions or practices. Here, in the place of theories of punishment, there are political and social philosophies. Some of them have within them elements having to do with desert. At any rate, they have within them elements that have to do with the actions of individuals taken as owed to Free Will. The truth of determinism requires at least an amendment of these philosophies. It also requires that we change our social institutions and practices in so far as they are owed to our image of origination. The response of affirmation will here also be a political response.

Is the Left Wing in politics less given to ideas of individual desert and more given to ideas of individual need? Is it then less given to attitudes and policies that have something of the assumption of Free Will in them? So you may suppose (cf. Honderich 1990). If that is so, should one part of the response of affirmation be a move to the Left in politics? We can pass by that bracing question.

12

AND YET . . .

THE preceding two chapters, about the response of Affirmation to determinism in one's own life and with respect to society, have been left more or less as they were in the first edition of this book, where they were the last two chapters. So you have read what was said originally of what follows on from our having two sets of attitudes with two thoughts of freedom in them, and from our two responses to determinism of Dismay and Intransigence. This was that one of the sets of attitudes is out of place and needs to be given up—the policy of Affirmation, *the* solution, as it was bravely said, to the problem of the consequences of determinism.

A good reason for leaving the two chapters as they were was to have the whole view put strongly. It may well all be true, as you will read again in my final line. If it has still not become an orthodoxy, it does not need to be hesitant. Certainly it must be as confident as the tired pair of traditions it replaces, Compatibilism and Incompatibilism. There is more need for unconventionality than conventionality in philosophy.

No doubt at all has crept into my mind about the falsehood of Compatibilism and Incompatibilism as against the truth of Attitudinism, or about the reality in our lives of the related pair of responses to determinism, Dismay and Intransigence. That is not quite the case with respect to the project of the giving up of one set of attitudes, the response of Affirmation. Here there are things you have just read in chapters 10 and 11 of which it can be said that some resolution was needed in order to leave them on the page without qualification.

Here, since the first edition, more thoughts and questions have got hold of me. They are not along the same lines. Nor are they along good lines proposed by other philosophers convinced of the need not merely to qualify Compatibilism and Incompatibilism, but to leave them behind (Double; Magill; Pereboom; Smilansky). It was remarked some way back that in a better world you would be reading a textbook of neuroscience rather than a chapter trying to summarize it. In a better world, you would also be giving your attention to these other departures from the cart-tracks of Hobbes and Bramhall. These various departures, akin to Attitudinism in their beginnings, are substantial and diverse enough to allow me to leave them unsummarized, and to merit your attention even in this lower world.

But for now, there is the fact that a general question can come up about the project of Affirmation. So it has happened with me at any rate. Indeed, what can come up is something that can seem to be on the way to a conviction. It is the question of whether a certain *sense of one's life* can have to do only with origination or Free Will, and nothing else, and thus in consistency with determinism we have to try to escape from it. Can this sense of one's life rest on some other ground instead? The sense in question has to do with more than one's moral responsibility, but that is part of it, and a place to start with these reflections.

If you settle down to think of your past life, to give it reflective attention, it can seem that you cannot avoid feeling responsible in a certain way for what you have done. This is likely to be more a matter of holding yourself responsible than crediting yourself with responsibility. To engage in autobiographical thinking of a serious sort, let alone the actual writing of an autobiography (Honderich 2001a), is surely to come to feel that your life has had in it patterns, actions, feelings and so on such that you would feel a lot better if they were missing. To get the sequence of your life into focus is surely to disapprove morally of yourself in something like the way that goes with accepting Free Will. It is to find retributive impulses in yourself against yourself. To get hold of the episodes of your past is surely to fall into or to be inclined to just that guilt contemplated earlier as something from which determinism should free us (p. 129).

That is a first point. It is close to what is maintained in a philosophical paper as important as any on determinism and freedom in the past century (P. F. Strawson). If the paper was a kind of defence of Compatibilism, it was also on the way to Attitudinism. One burden of it was that we have no chance of giving up certain attitudes to ourselves and others, including a kind of gratitude and resentment and also moral attitudes like the one now under consideration.

This particular kind of moral disapproval owed to autobiographical reflection, the special guilt, must at least at first seem to carry with it and depend on the image or idea of the initiation of actions inconsistent with determinism. It seems to carry with it what there is a lot of reason to despair of, an image of origination.

You cannot rescue yourself from the moral disapproval and guilt by the thought that you are merely *wanting* rather than *discovering* your past to have been inconsistent with determinism. You cannot readily pass off the moral disapproval as having to do with a desire rather than a truth. You are not wanting the credit of moral responsibility for past actions. To be of an ordinarily self-critical personality or culture, at any rate in the privacy of your own reflections, is to find yourself something like accused, not at all so agreeable as the promise of moral self-congratulation.

The situation is different, then, from the one in which philosophers of Free Will find themselves. They are desirous of a certain dignity for themselves as well as others, essentially a moral dignity, and some of them honestly admit it to be their desire (Kane; Ekstrom). It must place some question-mark over their conclusions, as remarked before (p. 78). The situation of self-accusation and guilt now under consideration is certainly different.

Will it be said that really to think about your life until now, to try to engage in it again, and as a result to find yourself in a state of self-doubt or worse, is merely to give evidence of being a certain kind of personality? An insecure personality? 'Neurotic', which is to say in that category most useful to the various plumbers of the depths of our minds? Putting aside the category from the plumbers, as I am inclined to do, it may still need to be admitted that an insecure reaction to one's past life is not a universal fact, not a law of human nature. That does not give me much pause. If all philosophy rested on laws of human nature, as distinct from facts of reasonable generality, there would be little philosophy of interest. It is my assumption that you, reader, can join me in my present troubled line of reflection. A habit of philosophical scepticism may help you, even if we do not often bring it to bear on our own lives.

That is not the end of the story about autobiographical

reflection, but only half of it. Our dealings with our pasts are not all judgemental, not all concerned with moral disapproval or approval. Often, if you get started on reflection about your past life, what you want is just to *understand*. How did it come about? How were those person-stages connected? How did I get where I got and become what I am? The aim is explanation, not judgement.

And, to come towards the second point of this chapter, the terrible fact is that you can deal with your past life in this way and fall into no uncertainty whatever about the proposition that everything that happened did have an explanation in the ordinary and indeed the only real sense. That is, it was an ordinary effect. Indeed you can *increase* your conviction of the truth of determinism. This has been my experience. Has it been owed to nothing arcane, but just to more knowledge of a subject-matter, recovery of a subject-matter? Has it been owed instead to a deeper fact—that there is no other way of understanding, of getting a subject-matter into conceptual good order, no other way than the way of real causes and effects?

At any rate, we have in these reflections come to a seeming contradiction. It is near to the one announced by the great Kant, also as a result of something about morality. Kant embraced determinism, in his way, but did not react to it in the Compatibilist way, by giving up indeterminism and restricting freedom to voluntariness. Far from it. Rather, he announced that he would have both determinism and indeterminism, both determinism and origination, by putting them in different places. Determinism in or for the phenomenal world or the world of our ordinary experience, indeterminism in the noumenal world, a world beyond and under our experience.

This Higher Compatibilism, entirely at odds with ordinary or mundane Compatibilism, must be hopeless. A distinction between two worlds or two conceptions of *the* world is of course possible, and has a number of philosophical versions, several of them less metaphysical than Kant's. But there seems no hope whatever of locating indeterminism and freedom significantly in only one of them, and certainly no hope for taking it out of the experienced world entirely. In any case, since what is undetermined and free must in some sense turn up in both worlds, it is impossible to see that the contradiction is actually escaped. Certainly there can be no good sense in the sort of philosophical speculation that supposes there can be two ways of seeing the same things, two perspectives on them, such that what is true about these same things in one perspective can safely be contradicted in the other perspective.

Is it conceivable, to come towards a third and the main point in these reflections, in fact a question, that some philosophical idea as radical as Kant's can have a better hope of dealing with the seeming contradiction? Is it conceivable that some entire departure from our philosophical habits can make it possible to persist with determinism and yet also to persist in a moral attitude that has been taken as needing the support of indeterminism and origination? In particular, is it conceivable that we can by some idea or other persist in certain attitudes, which do indeed seem tied up with the obscure and factitious machinery of origination—*persist in these attitudes without recourse to the machinery of origination and in all ways consistently with determinism?*

Something else needs attention before we look at this main question.[1] Something else, in fact, changes the question significantly. At the start, it was said that autobiographical reflection can raise a question about a basis of a sense of one's life. An idea of oneself as morally responsible is a part of this sense of a life, but only a part. This sense of one's life has to do at least as much or maybe more with a thing different from morality.

It is my idea and feeling that in my life I have *been my own man.* What I mean, by this somewhat different use of a common piece of English, is that I have been one with very many others, almost all of us in what is called Western culture. And it is not political correctness that makes it necessary to add that being one's own man in this sense is no different from being your own woman. The piece of English in my use of it of catches hold of more lives than particularly characterful or brave ones. In that better world remarked on several times before, there would be time to try to elaborate what it is to be one's own man or woman. Use might be made of talk of *autonomy*, where that is taken to be something somehow different from freedom.

To come to another plainer summary of this non-moral self-perception, let me quickly say only that there has been some

---

[1]   This main question is put mistakenly, I see, on pp. 398–9 of my autobiographical book *Philosopher: A Kind of Life*. What is needed by way of a new idea is certainly not a new conception of origination as we have been understanding it.

individuality about my life. There has been a uniqueness that can seem to be in conflict with my life's having been a sequence of causal circumstances. This individuality is certainly not a matter of my being significantly different from others in terms of character or personality. Each of at least many of us, paradoxically, is individual in this way. It is not too much to say that each of us stands apart from others and from everything else.

So—I can have a sense of my life that consists in a certain feeling of moral responsibility and also an idea, separate from morality, of an individuality or uniqueness. Does it have other sides? These two will be enough for our reflections. This sense of my life, to continue, suggests a source that it cannot really have, a source in the murky machinery of origination, once characterized as panicky metaphysics (P. F. Strawson). Can it be that there is another ground, very different, for this sense? It would be agreeable to have a confident and developed idea of such a ground to report to you, but I do not have that.

What can be done, first, is to indicate how radical a departure from our habits I have in mind in our looking for such a ground. An example will help. Something clear is needed, since recent philosophers of Free Will have also been inclined to call for new thinking, and been humanly inclined to suppose that they have done some (Kane). This new thinking, from a perspective outside of their struggle, is more of the same. This is not the sort of thing I have in mind. The departure that may be needed in connection with determinism and freedom, and in particular in connection with determinism and a sense of a life as individual, is in fact a kind of change of subject.

My example will be an alteration in thinking on the nature of consciousness, or at least perceptual consciousness. This idea of mine, for such it is, may be followed by a like alteration with respect to reflective and affective consciousness (p. 77). These, you may remember, roughly have to do not with seeing and the like but with kinds of thinking and desiring.

There may also be better reason for attending to this idea. It is that it seems possible that the new thinking that is needed with determinism and our senses of our lives will actually have to do with the nature of consciousness. It may have to do, yet more fundamentally, with consciousness and the nature of reality. It may be that the true resolution of the problem of determinism and our senses of our lives is to be found not in moral philosophy, and not in the philosophy of mind narrowly understood, but in metaphysics and epistemology, these being understood as philosophical concerns with the nature of reality and our part of it and our role in it. It may be, even, that the particular new thinking on consciousness will do something to resolve the problem of a basis of our senses of our lives.

To go back before we go forward, the nature of consciousness first had our attention when we were concerned with a first part of the theory of determinism. We supposed that consciousness is a reality, and that conscious or mental events take up space and time, and that consciousness is distinguished from all else by the character referred to as its subjectivity, the most fundamental fact about it. To these secure suppositions were added others as secure. There is a necessary connection of some kind between our events of consciousness and our neural events—psychoneural intimacy is a fact. There is also the fact of causal connections between mental events and earlier and later non-mental events—the events of the glass of wine being on the waiter's tray before me and the movement of my arm towards it. These later connections give rise to the mind–body problem (chapter 3).

As a result of more or less attention to one or more of these considerations, philosophers and others have come to a small number of kinds of answer to the question of the nature of consciousness. Their many answers can be reduced, in my opinion, to the following few kinds.

Some philosophers, including many concerned above all with the mind–body problem, at bottom the problem of how non-mental events of neurons can be in causal connection with mental events, have persisted with the materialist answer that the mental events are the same. They have only the properties of neural events. Hobbes in the seventeenth century was right in taking consciousness to be cells.

A second lot of philosophers and fellow-workers, much larger, have coated the pill of this materialism by concentrating on the aforementioned relations between mental events and earlier and later events—here we have Functionalism, a philosophically speculative kind of Cognitive Science or Artificial Intelligence (pp. 27–8). These labourers, as I see it, have left the materialism as unswallowable as it has always been.

A third kind of answer to the question of the nature of consciousness, perhaps presupposed in much of neuroscience, is the idea that mental events have physical properties, but physical properties as yet unknown. They have properties that are not yet part of neuroscience and not around the corner either. It is not only the obscurity of this view that makes it as hopeless.

These three kinds of answer to the question of the nature of consciousness are to me and others hopeless because they can give no adequate account of subjectivity. That is close to saying they give no adequate account of the very nature of consciousness. There is that great difference between your consciousness and the existence of cells, coated cells and future cells. A fourth kind of answer, associated historically with Descartes but close to all ordinary unreflective thinking about consciousness, is at first more promising. It transpires, however, that it is mainly promising in its mystery. This is Immaterialism, often misleadingly called Mind–Body Dualism.

What it comes to at bottom is that consciousness is stuff that is out of space. It exists, and is had by persons, but takes up no space. It is a matter of a substance or thing, a substantial self or subject, and is absolutely different from the rest of what exists, which is matter. An overwhelming problem for Immaterialism is of course the mind–body problem. It is hard to dissent from the consensus that Immaterialism is destroyed by it. How can something without any dimensions, or perhaps even locality, cause my arm to move?

Our look at the nature of consciousness in connection with Mind–Brain Determinism in chapter 3 did not try to do better than these four kinds of answer to the question of the nature of consciousness. As recalled a moment ago, we came only to the proposition that conscious or mental events, whatever their nature, are in nomic connection with our neural events. That was sufficient to our needs. Now we have reasons to look at another answer to the question of the nature of consciousness, anyway an answer to the question of the nature of perceptual consciousness.

What is it for you now to be aware of the room you are in? *It is for the room in a way to exist.* That answer can be shown not to be merely a rhetorical way of saying that you are aware of the room. It is not a non-analysis. Rather, the claim that your perceptual consciousness consists in a kind of existence of a world consists in the claim that there is a certain state of affairs, certainly not in your head.

It is a particular state of affairs consisting of things, reasonably called chairs and the like, being in space and time and being dependent on other facts. It is dependent on another world, roughly speaking the relevant atoms, and it also has another dependency, on your neurons in particular. The world in question is anterior to the perceived physical world as we define it. That public world is the one dependent both on atoms and crucially on no individual in particular but on all of us, above all on our shared perceptual apparatus and our shared conceptual scheme. That we make such a contribution to this reality has been plain since the seventeenth century (Honderich 2001d).

In this analysis of perceptual consciousness, a general physicalism is in a way held onto, or not far departed from, and the mystery of non-physical stuff somehow in the head is absolutely abandoned. But what has attracted so many to this stuff, its vanishing recommendation, is delivered to us by something else. What we get, above all, in the idea of Perceptual Consciousness as Existence, is the fact of subjectivity made real and clear.

What is subjective about perceptual consciousness is that for each of us our perceptual consciousness is a personal world different from the perceived part of the physical world and other worlds, and a world ordinarily open to and dependent on just one subject. Your perceptual world's dependency, putting aside its dependency on the world underneath, the world of atoms and the like, is not a dependency on subjects generally but a dependency only on your neural existence. That is not to say, to repeat, that we have got far from physicalism. Your world, it can be argued, is no less 'real' than the perceived part of the physical world. If the latter is not to be made into mysterious stuff in the head by its dependency on persons generally, why should your world of perceptual consciousness be degraded into such stuff by its dependency on you?

You are not likely to be persuaded of this doctrine, Consciousness as Existence, or rather Perceptual Consciousness as Existence, by a few words delivered on the wing. In any case, as remarked, it needs to have added to it related accounts of reflective and affective consciousness. The lesser of my two lesser aims in stating it baldly, to recall it, is to indicate something of the order of differentness of thought that may be needed if we are to make a better escape than that of Attitudinism and Affirmation from three centuries of impasse in the philosophy of determinism and freedom. We need to get as far from origination as Consciousness as Existence is from the four standard kinds of answer to the question of the nature of consciousness.

My second reason for turning our attention to Perceptual Consciousness as Existence was that the new thinking that seems to be needed with determinism and our senses of our lives may well have to do with the nature of consciousness. Given what has been said of the subjectivity of perceptual consciousness, according to our doctrine, little needs to be said of its recommendation. It promises to see all of consciousness in such a way that it is something that may explain your sense of your life, without aid from indeterminism.

That is, it explains your sense of your life as a sense of something for which you are accountable and also something that is individual and indeed unique in another way or ways. For you to be conscious is for much more to exist than something or other in your head. (It always was at least uncomfortable to think of consciousness as something literally inside a head.) For you to be conscious is for a unique world in a way to exist. It can be added that it is on such worlds that the physical world in its two parts rests. We get to the physical world by way of our unique worlds.

You are excused if you say that this is no longer English philosophy, no longer the dominant philosophy in the language of the English-speaking world. It is high reasoning or deep thinking, assigned earlier to French and German philosophy (p. 105). Well, as I have been saying, it may be time for another change, whether or not in the French or German direction. You can arrive by English steps at the need for another kind of progress.

Not to be faint-hearted, let me leave you, particularly the one or two open-minded postgraduate students of the age, with one other thought. It is another indication of the extent to which we may need to abandon the philosophy of determinism and freedom as we have and have had it and start up again in this new millennium. It may also actually be of use with the problem of determinism and freedom, and in particular another basis for our senses of our lives.

A causal circumstance, you may remember, is a set of events that necessitated an effect. We typically isolate and elevate one of those events and say it caused the effect, or indeed was the cause of the effect—as against another mere condition of the effect, another event in the causal circumstance. This cause may be the human action in the set, and will hardly ever be so ordinary as the presence of oxygen. In general it is the event that most interests us or the event that it is in our interests to isolate (chapter 2).

Suppose you set about explaining something in a life, perhaps a pattern of it or a culmination of it. You take the pattern or culmination to be the effect of a causal sequence, this being a sequence or past array of causal circumstances. You can now do the further thing of isolating a cause in each of the causal circumstances or maybe just some of them. This gives you what can be called a *causal line* within and from the beginning of the sequence to the pattern or culmination. It may be that this is much of what is had in mind by philosophers who speak of a *narrative* in connection with a life (MacIntyre).

There is a problem about isolating a single condition in a causal circumstance and dignifying it as the cause. The problem, a paradox if you will, is that in a clear sense this cause is no more explanatory of the effect than any other condition in the causal circumstance. All are required or necessary conditions. But the cause seems to be exactly that—*more explanatory*. That is exactly what is conveyed by calling it the cause. Evidently there is the very same problem about a causal line. In one clear sense it cannot be more explanatory than any other chosen succession of items or states, say presences of oxygen. But it *is* more explanatory, isn't it (Honderich 2001a)?

What this comes to is that the culmination of a life, say, is a matter of plain determinism, but there seems also to be the possibility of some kind of explanation of it that is different in kind. Some kind of departure from determinism, or unexpected addition to it. At any rate there is a problem or paradox here. The putative explanation would be consistent with determinism, indeed within it, but different in kind from ordinary causal explanation—ordinary explanation of an event by a causal circumstance. I have wondered, unsuccessfully so far, if the thing is worth reflection in connection with determinism and the attitudes in which we can find ourselves persisting—determinism and a sense of one's life.

It may be that we shall get nowhere. It may be, despite what has been said, that there is no need to try. Your sense of your life as individual, if you too have one, may be a kind of illusion. You may be no more than a victim of that process of acculturation mentioned earlier, that one that has much to do with Western religions and begins with our mothers. You may have had both an ungrounded feeling of moral responsibility imposed on you and also a mistakenly enlarged sense of your existence and your importance. It could be that there is no truth that gives us what I have been calling our senses of our lives. We are just giving in to mother.

If it comes to seem so to me, I will pass beyond Compatibilism and Incompatibilism only to the security of the attitudinal doctrine and our two ideas and to the hope of the project of affirmation. They may be truth and reason, if not perfect contentment.

Glossary

Action Determinism theories of how or why our actions come about—they are effects of certain causal sequences, not originated

active intention an intention that immediately gives rise to and may accompany an action, sometimes called a volition or act of will

Affirmation a response to determinism that involves trying to give up things inconsistent with it, for example a kind of life-hope, partly by seeing the value of what doesn't have to be given up and by seeing any compensations of determinism

attitude usually an approving or disapproving thought of something, such as one's future or an action by somebody else, where the thought is bound up with desire and somehow feelingful

Attitudinism Compatibilism and Incompatibilism share the proposition that we have a single and settled concept of freedom; attitudinism is the opposed proposition that the fact of our having two kinds or families of attitudes, including life-hopes and moral disapproval, proves that we have two different conceptions of freedom

behaviourism family of doctrines, some more radical than others, characterizing consciousness and mentality in terms of behaviour

causal circumstance a set of conditions or events that necessitates something later, an effect, and hence is in a kind of nomic connection with it; hence a causal circumstance makes it impossible that any event other than the effect will occur

causal connection a familiar form of nomic connection where one of the things connected, a causal circumstance, comes before the other, the effect

causal sequence a chain or unbroken or gapless series of events, such that each except the first is the effect of the immediately preceding one, and hence of all the other preceding ones; thus all of these, including of course the last, are necessitated by the initial causal circumstance

cause one event or condition within a causal circumstance, the one singled out for special attention, sometimes a human action, sometimes an unusual event

chance event   see random event

cognitive science   a cluster of sciences attempting to explain what consciousness and thinking or cognition are and how they come about

Compatibilism   the doctrine, about what is taken to be our single and settled concept of freedom, that choices, decisions, and actions can be both free in this way and also determined; the terms 'free' and 'determined' (or 'free' and 'caused') are logically compatible terms; the doctrine rests on taking freedom as consisting in voluntariness and not involving origination

conditional statements   a subclass of 'if–then'-statements, typified by 'If the match is struck, it will light' but not by various other 'if–then'-statements, including 'If he's bachelor, he's unmarried'

consequences or implications of determinism   the results of it or what it means in terms of life-hopes, personal feelings, confidence about knowledge, moral approval and disapproval or moral responsibility, right actions, judgements of persons, and social institutions and practices

determinism   often, as in this book, a theory that all our mental events, including choices and decisions, and also our actions, are effects of certain things and therefore have to happen or are necessitated, and cannot be owed to origination

determinism, the three parts of the theory of it in this book   (1) mental events are nomically connected with simultaneous neural events; (2) these are the effects of certain causal chains; (3) actions are also effects

Dismay   the sad response to determinism (contrasted with Intransigence) of thinking that something, for example, life-hopes, are destroyed or must be entirely given up because determinism is true, or that this is the likely prospect because determinism is likely to be true

effect   an event necessitated or guaranteed by a causal circumstance

embraced desires   desires into which the person really enters, for example the desire to have a job, as against reluctant desires owed to a frustrating circumstance, for example an unemployed man's grudgingly wanting to watch television to while away the time

epiphenomenalism   the doctrine that mental events, unlike neural events, don't cause and aren't parts of the explanations of other mental events and actions, but are just side-effects of neural events

free choice, decision, or action (1) one that was voluntary, and hence consistent with determinism's being true; or (2) one that was voluntary but also originated or owed to Free Will, and hence inconsistent with determinism

freedom a state or condition or possession having to do with choosing and acting voluntarily, or choosing and acting voluntarily but also out of origination

Free Will a kind or part of freedom that is or rests on our supposed personal power to originate choices and thus actions—i.e. **origination as a power;** sometimes used more generally

functionalism doctrines that mental events are whatever events have a certain function, i.e. stand in causal or other relations to earlier and later events, these often referred to as input and output

Identity Theory the theory, which can take many forms, that the mind is numerically identical with the brain—there is just one thing in question—or that each mental event is identical with a simultaneous neural event; sometimes thought to be either a piece of nonsense or truistic

inactive intention an intention to perform an action later, which does not immediately result in the action

Incompatibilism the doctrine, about what is taken to be our single and settled concept of freedom, that choices, decisions, and actions cannot be both free in this way and also determined; the terms 'free' and 'determined' are incompatible or inconsistent terms; the doctrine rests on taking freedom to involve origination

indeterminism often, as in this book, the view that at least some of our mental events, above all our choices and decisions, are not effects in the way that the opposite view of determinism supposes; strictly speaking, they are chance or random events; but it may be added—although this is no part of indeterminism itself—that they are originated and thus saved from being random or chance events in some other sense

Initiation Determinism theories of how or why mental events and their associated neural events come about or are initiated—they are effects of certain causal sequences, not originated

initiation of an action the beginning or source of an action, either in voluntariness or in both voluntariness and origination

intention a complex or bundle of a desire and various beliefs, and, in the case of an active intention, a puzzling executive element

interactionism sometimes the view that a neural event may be the whole cause of a later mental event, and a mental event the whole cause of a later neural event

Intransigence the tough response to determinism (contrasted with Dismay) of thinking that some things, for example life-hopes, are untouched by it

lawlike connection see nomic connection

Libertarianism the doctrine, also called Free Will, that freedom rightly understood includes a power of origination, inconsistent with determinism, and that we do in fact have this power; libertarianism or Free Will thus consists in Incompatibilism, which is the effect that only one of two things can be the case, and then an account of which one is the case

life-hope a large hope fundamental to a stage of an individual's life, perhaps his or her main attitude to the future, involving thoughts of future actions taken as voluntary, or as voluntary and originated

mental or conscious events real events in time and space having a character of subjectivity, somehow related to neural events

micro-level the level of small particles of matter theorized about in physics, as distinct from the macro-level, which includes everything larger than the particles, including neurons and neural events

Mind–Brain Determinism theories holding that minds (or consciousness or mental events) are somehow connected with brains (or neural events) in a nomic or lawlike way

moral responsibility the term is used in various ways in connection with holding people morally responsible, which is being somehow morally disapproving of them for a wrong action, or crediting people with moral responsibility, which is being morally approving of them for a right action

morally responsible sometimes the term means free in one or the other of the two ways in having performed a particular action, and therefore open to being held morally responsible for it in one of two ways or credited with moral responsibility for it in one of two ways

near-determinism the view that while there is indeterminism at the micro-level, the level of small particles, there is still determinism at the macro-level, which includes neural events and everything with which we are ordinarily familiar

necessitated event an effect or else another event in nomic connection
with something else

neural events events that have only neural properties, i.e. electrochemical
properties

nomic connection in one fundamental form the connection between two
things such that if or since one occurred, whatever else had been the
case, the other would still have occurred

nomic correlates two things in nomic connection, but neither occurring
before the other, and hence not a causal circumstance and its effect

originated choice or action one owed to the individual's power of
origination

origination as an event or occurrence it is the emergence or bringing-about
of a mental event such as a decision or an action (1) in such a way that
the opposite mental event or action might at that moment just as well
have occurred although the person had remained in every respect the
same and his or her situation had remained the same, and (2) in such a
way that the person had control of the mental event or action and can
in a certain way be held responsible for it or credited with responsibility
for it. Because of (1), origination is inconsistent with ordinary causation
and determinism; because of (2), an originated action is not merely an
uncaused or chance event; origination is indeterminism plus something
else

origination as a power our supposed personal power of giving rise to
originations as occurrences, often called Free Will

originator the entity, sometimes also called a self, which is said to originate
mental events

psychoneural intimacy the fact that a mental event is in some very close
connection, a necessary connection, with a simultaneous neural event

psychoneural pair a mental event and the simultaneous neural event with
which it is in nomic connection, often a cause or causal circumstance
for a later such pair or an action

random event event not caused by anything, and therefore without an
explanation of why it actually occurred, even if it was probable

reluctant desires see embraced desires

response in this book, one of three reactions to thinking of something,
for example life-hopes, on the assumption that determinism is or is
likely to be true—the three reactions being Dismay, Intransigence, and
Affirmation

responsibility see moral responsibility

Union Theory the theory that a neural event and a simultaneous mental event are not identical or one thing, but the neural event necessitates the mental event and the mental event is necessary to the neural event

usual cause something that usually results in an event, distinct from a causal circumstance

Utilitarianism the doctrine or morality, which comes in several forms, that the right action, policy, or institution is the one that is most likely to produce the greatest total of satisfaction, or the greatest balance of satisfaction over dissatisfaction

voluntariness in general, the property of a choice or action that is its being in accordance with the agent's true nature and his or her desires

voluntary choice or action always one that is in accordance with the agent's true nature and his or her desires, but likely to be described a bit differently if the action is being thought of in connection with holding someone else responsible, say, rather than in connection with one's own future actions

A Note on Further Reading

The chapters of this book, except for the last one, have the same subjects as the chapters of my much longer and more scholarly *A Theory of Determinism: The Mind, Neuroscience, and Life-Hopes*— which became the two paperbacks *Mind and Brain* and *The Consequences of Determinism*. Readers of the present book who want more detail and qualification can look up parts of these predecessors. They are clear enough, but they don't leave anything out. Reading through them requires diligence.

You may be interested in brief introductory books other than the one you are reading. To my mind, you are likely to get more from struggling with the real stuff—the philosophy of determinism and freedom as it is, not potted or watered down. For an excellent anthology of twenty-six real articles by the leading figures in the field and others, there is Kane's *The Oxford Handbook of Free Will*. It more or less supplanted all other such collections.

Do you say brief introductions have their place? Well, you can find articles that give overviews of the whole subject and also of the various parts of it (causation, moral responsibility, etc.) in good philosophical encyclopedias. Try the ten-volume *Routledge Encyclopedia of Philosophy* edited by Craig and the one-volume *Oxford Companion to Philosophy* edited by me; also Audi's one-volume *Cambridge Dictionary of Philosophy*; although it is older, Edwards's two-volume *Encyclopedia of Philosophy* is very good. Remember, though, that contributors to stately reference works are not godlike in independence and objectivity, but have their own fish to fry. Some promote their own views more than others do.

Small books of brief introduction to the whole subject of determinism and freedom are Ekstrom's *Free Will: A Philosophical Study*, which gets technical in defence of Incompatibilism, and McFee's *Free Will*, also idiosyncratic. A little more to my own taste, but not so up to date, are Trusted, *Freewill and Responsibility* and D. J. O'Connor, *Free Will*.

As remarked above, earlier anthologies, each including various philosophers, were more or less supplanted by *The Oxford Handbook of Free Will*. Still, there are some that have the recommendation of including somewhat older pieces that may survive longer, and also classical pieces by philosophers of past centuries. These include Hook's *Determinism and Freedom in the Age of Modern Science*, Berofsky's *Free Will and Determinism*, my own *Essays on Freedom of Action*, Lehrer's *Freedom and Determinism*, Timothy O'Connor's *Agents, Causes, Events*, Pears's *Freedom and the Will* (from an earlier round of the debate), Morgenbesser and Walsh's *Free Will*, and Watson's *Free Will*.

Whole books by single authors, argumentative and readable but not so introductory as the brief introductions just mentioned, are Berofsky's *Freedom From Necessity*, Dennett's *Elbow Room*, Double's *The Non-Reality of Free Will*, Fischer's *The Metaphysics of Free Will*, Frankfurt's *The Importance of What We Care About*, Ginet's *On Action*, Magill's *Freedom and Experience*, Mele's *Autonomous Agents*, Timothy O'Connor's *Persons and Causes*, Pereboom's *Living Without Free Will*, Galen Strawson's *Freedom and Belief*, Thorp's *Free Will: A Defence against Neurophysiological Determinism*, van Inwagen's *An Essay on Free Will*, and Weatherford's *The Implications of Determinism*.

Bibliography

ADLER, M. (1958). *The Idea of Freedom: A Dialectical Examination of the Conceptions of Freedom*. New York, Doubleday.

ALBERT, D. (1992). *Quantum Mechanics and Experience*. Cambridge, MA, Harvard University Press.

ANSCOMBE, G. E. M. (1963), *Intention*. Ithaca, Cornell University Press.

—— (1972). 'The Causation of Action', address to Institut International de Philosophie, Cambridge.

—— (1981). 'Causality and Determination', *The Collected Philosophical Papers of G. E. M. Anscombe*, vol. 2. Minneapolis, University of Minnesota Press.

ARMSTRONG, D. (1983). *What Is a Law of Nature?* Cambridge, Cambridge University Press.

AUDI, R. (1995). *The Cambridge Dictionary of Philosophy*. Cambridge and New York, Cambridge University Press.

AUSTIN, J. L. (1961). 'Ifs and Cans', in his *Philosophical Papers*. Oxford, Oxford University Press.

BELL, J. S. (1987). *Speakable and Unspeakable in Quantum Mechanics*. Cambridge, Cambridge University Press.

BENENSON, F. C. (1984). *Probability, Objectivity and Evidence*. London, Routledge.

BEROFSKY, B. (ed.) (1966). *Free Will and Determinism*. New York, Harper.

—— (1987). *Freedom From Necessity: The Metaphysical Basis of Responsibility*. London and New York, Routledge.

BISHOP, R. (2002). 'Chaos, Indeterminism and Free Will', in Kane 2002a.

BLOCK, N. (ed.) (1980a). *Readings in Philosophy of Psychology*, 2 vols. Cambridge, MA, Harvard University Press.

—— (1980b). 'What is Functionalism?', in Block 1980a.

BOHM, D. (1957). *Causality and Chance*. London, Routledge and Kegan Paul.

—— (1980). *Wholeness and the Implicate Order*. London, Routledge and Kegan Paul.

BOHM, D. and HILEY, B. (1993). *The Undivided Universe*. London, Routledge.

BOYLE, J. M., CRISEZ, G., and TOLLEFSEN, O. (1976). *Free Choice: A Self-Referential Argument*. Notre Dame, Notre Dame University Press.

BRAMHALL, J. (1844). 'A Defence of True Liberty', in *The Works of John Bramhall*. Oxford, John Henry Parker.

BRATMAN, M. (1987). *Intention, Plans and Practical Reason*. Cambridge, Cambridge University Press.

BUB, J. (1997). *Interpreting the Quantum World*. Cambridge, Cambridge University Press.

—— (1998). 'Quantum Measurement Problem', in Craig 1998.

BUTTERFIELD, J. (1998). 'Determinism and Indeterminism', in Craig 1998.

CAMPBELL, K. (1970). *Body and Mind*. London, Macmillan.

CARLSON, N. R. (1994). *Physiology of Behaviour*. Boston, Alleyn and Bacon.

CARTWRIGHT, N. (1998). 'Causation', in Craig 1998.

CHISHOLM, R. M. (1976). 'The Agent as Cause', in M. Brand and D. Walton (eds), *Action Theory*. Dordrecht, Reidel.

—— (1995). 'Agents, Causes and Events: The Problem of Free Will', in T. O'Connor 1995a.

CHOMSKY, N. (1971). Review of B. F. Skinner, *Beyond Freedom and Dignity*. *New York Review of Books*.

CHURCHLAND, P. (1986). *Neurophilosophy*. Cambridge, MA, MIT Press.

CHURCHLAND, P. M. (1981). 'Eliminative Materialism and the Propositional Attitudes', *Journal of Philosophy*.

—— (1984). *Matter and Consciousness*. Cambridge, MA, MIT Press.

CLARKE, R. (1995). 'Towards a Credible Agent-Causal Account of Free Will', in O'Connor 1995.

COHEN, G. A. (1978). *Karl Marx's Theory of History: A Defence*. Oxford, Oxford University Press.

COHEN, L. J. (1989). *An Introduction to the Philosophy of Induction and Probability*. Oxford, Oxford University Press.

COTMAN, C. W. and McGAUGH, J. W. (1980). *Behavioural Neuroscience*. New York, Academic Press.

CRAIG, E. (ed.) (1998). *Routledge Encyclopedia of Philosophy*. London, Routledge.

CUSHING, J. T. (1994). *Quantum Theory: Historical Contingency and the Copenhagen Hegemony*. Chicago, University of Chicago Press.

CUSHING, J. T. and McMULLIN, E. (eds) (1989). *Philosophical Consequences of Quantum Theory*. Notre Dame, Notre Dame University Press.

DANTO, A. (1973). *Analytical Philosophy of Action*. Cambridge, Cambridge University Press.

DAVIDSON, D. (1980). 'Mental Events', in his *Essays on Actions and Events*. Oxford, Oxford University Press.

—— (1993). 'Thinking Causes', in Heil & Mele 1993.

DAVIES, L. H. (1972). 'They Deserve to Suffer', *Analysis*.

DAVIES, P. C. W. (1979). *Quantum Mechanics*. London, Routledge.

—— (1986). *The Forces of Nature*. Cambridge, Cambridge University Press.

DAVIS, L. (1979). *A Theory of Action*. Englewood Cliffs, Prentice Hall.

DAVIS, W. A. (1983). 'The Two Senses of Desire', *Philosophical Studies*.

—— (1984). 'A Causal Theory of Intending', *American Philosophical Quarterly*.

DAY, J. P. (1991). *Hope: A Philosophical Inquiry*. Helsinki, Alcateeminen Kirjatcanppa.

DENNETT, D. C. (1984). *Elbow Room: The Varieties of Free Will Worth Wanting*. Oxford, Oxford University Press.

—— (1988). 'Coming to Terms with the Determined'. Review of Honderich, *A Theory of Determinism*. *Times Literary Supplement*, November 4–10.

—— (1991). *Consciousness Explained*. New York, Little Brown.

d'ESPAGNAT, B. (1995). *Veiled Reality*. New York, Addison Wesley.

DOUBLE, R. (1991). *The Non-Reality of Free Will*. New York, Oxford University Press.

—— (1996a). *Metaphilosophy and Free Will*. Oxford, Oxford University Press.

—— (1996b). 'Honderich on the Consequences of Determinism', *Philosophy and Phenomenological Research*.

—— (1997). 'Misdirection on the Free Will Problem', *American Philosophical Quarterly*.

—— (1999). 'In Defence of the Smart Aleck: A Reply to Ted Honderich', *Journal of Philosophical Research*.

DUFF, R. A. (1986). *Trials and Punishments*. Cambridge, Cambridge University Press.

—— (1998). 'Crime and Punishment', in Craig 1998.

EARMAN, J. (1986). *A Primer on Determinism*. Dordrecht, Reidel.

ECCLES, J. C. and Popper, K. (1977). *The Self and its Brain*. Berlin, Springer.

EDWARDS, P. (ed.) (1967a). *Encyclopedia of Philosophy*. New York, Macmillan.

—— (1967b). 'The Meaning and Value of Life', in Edwards 1967a.

EELLS, E. (1991). *Probabilistic Causality*. Cambridge: Cambridge University Press.

EINSTEIN, A., PODOLSKY, B., and ROSEN, N. (1935). 'Can Quantum Mechanical Description of Reality Be Considered Complete?', *Physical Review*.

EKSTROM, L. W. (2000). *Free Will: A Philosophical Study*. Boulder, Westview.

ENGELS, F. (1978) [1934]. *Anti-Duhring*, trans. E. Burns. London, Lawrence and Wishart.

FISCHER, J. (1986). *Moral Responsibility*. Ithaca, NY, Cornell University Press.

—— (1994). *The Metaphysics of Free Will: A Study of Control*. Oxford, Blackwell.

—— (1996). 'A New Compatibilism', *Philosophical Topics*.

—— (2000). 'The Significance of Free Will', *Philosophy and Phenomenological Research*.

FISCHER, J. and RAVIZZA, M. (1993). *Perspectives on Moral Responsibility*. Ithaca, Cornell University Press.

—— (1995). 'When the Will Is Free', in T. O'Connor, 1995a.

—— (1998). *Responsibility and Control: A Theory of Moral Responsibility*. Cambridge, Cambridge University Press.

FLANAGAN, O. J. (1984). *The Science of the Mind*. Cambridge, MA, Bradford.

FRANKFURT, H. (1969). 'Alternate Possibilities and Moral Responsibility', *Journal of Philosophy*.

—— (1971). 'Freedom of the Will and the Concept of a Person', *Journal of Philosophy*.

—— (1988). *The Importance of What We Care About*. New York, Cambridge University Press.

—— (1999). *Necessity, Volition and Love*. Cambridge, Cambridge University Press.

GINET, K. (1990). *On Action*. Cambridge, Cambridge University Press.

—— (1995). 'Reasons Explanations of Actions: An Incompatibilist Account', in T. O'Connor 1995a.

—— (2002). 'Reasons Explanations of Actions: Causalist Versus Non-Causalist Accounts', in Kane 2002a.

GOLDMAN, A. H. (1979). 'The Paradox of Punishment', *Philosophy and Public Affairs*.

GOLDMAN, A. I. (1970). *A Theory of Human Action*. Englewood Cliffs, Prentice Hall.

GREENFIELD, S. A. (1997). *The Human Brain: A Guided Tour*. London, Weidenfeld and Nicolson.

—— (2000). *The Private Life of the Brain*. New York, Wiley.

HALDANE, J. B. (1932). *The Inequality of Man*. London, Gollancz.

—— (1954). 'I Repent An Error', *Literary Guide*.

HAMPSHIRE, S. (1959). *Thought and Action*. London, Chatto and Windus.

—— (1965). *Freedom of the Individual*. London, Chatto and Windus.

—— (1966). 'The Uses of Speculation', *Encounter*.

HAMPSHIRE, S. (1972). *Freedom of Mind and Other Essays*. Oxford, Oxford University Press.

HANNAN, B. (2001). 'Schopenhauer on Freedom of the Will and Mental Causation', Proceedings Inland North West Philosophy Conference.

HEIL, J. (1998). *Philosophy of Mind: A Contemporary Introduction*. London, Routledge.

HEIL, J. and MELE, A. (eds) (1993). *Mental Causation*. Oxford, Oxford University Press.

HOBBES, T. (1962). 'Of Liberty and Necessity', in W. Molesworth (ed.), *The English Works of Thomas Hobbes*, vol. 5. London, Scientia Aalen.

HONDERICH, T. (1973). *Essays on Freedom of Action*. London, Routledge.

—— (1981). 'The Problem of Well-Being and the Principle of Equality', *Mind*.

—— (1982). 'Against Teleological Historical Determinism', *Inquiry*.

—— (1984a, 1989). *Punishment: The Supposed Justifications*. Harmondsworth, Penguin, and Cambridge, Polity.

—— (1984b). 'Smith and the Champion of Mauve', *Analysis*.

—— (1988). *A Theory of Determinism: The Mind, Neuroscience, and Life-Hopes*. Oxford, Oxford University Press. 1990 reissued as *Mind and Brain* and *The Consequences of Determinism*. Oxford, Oxford University Press.

—— (1990). *Conservatism*. London, Hamish Hamilton, Penguin.

—— (1994a). 'Functionalism, Identity Theories, the Union Theory', in Walker and Szubka.

—— (1994b). 'Seeing Things', *Synthese*.

—— (1995). 'Consciousness, Neural Functionalism, Real Subjectivity', *American Philosophical Quarterly*.

—— (1995). *The Oxford Companion to Philosophy*. Oxford, Oxford University Press.

—— (1997). 'Consciousness as Existence', in Anthony O'Hear, ed., *Current Issues in the Philosophy of Mind*, Royal Institute of Philosophy Lectures. Cambridge, Cambridge University Press.

—— (1999). 'Consciousness as Existence Again', in *Proceedings of the Twentieth World Congress of Philosophy*, vol. 9, Philosophy of Mind, ed. B. Elevitch. Bowling Green, Philosophy Documentation Center.

—— (2001a). *Philosopher: A Kind of Life*. London and New York, Routledge.

—— (2001b). 'Mind the Guff: A Response to John Searle', *Journal of Consciousness Studies*.

—— (2001c). 'Consciousness and Inner Tubes: Review of David Papineau's *Introducing Consciousness*', *Journal of Consciousness Studies*.

—— (2001d), 'Consciousness and the End of Intentionality', in Anthony O'Hear, ed., *Philosophy at the New Millennium*, Royal Institute of Philosophy Lectures. Cambridge, Cambridge University Press.

—— (2002). 'Determinism as True, Compatibilism and Incompatibilism as False, and the Real Problem', in Kane 2002a.

HOOK, S. (1961). *Determinism and Freedom in the Age of Modern Science*. New York, Collier.

HOOKER, C. A. (1998). 'Laws, Natural', in Craig 1998.

HORNSBY, J. (1998). 'Action', in Craig 1998.

HUME, D. (1748 [1902]), *An Enquiry Concerning Human Understanding*, ed. L. A. Selby-Bigge. Oxford, Clarendon.

JACKSON, F. (1982). 'Epiphenomenal Qualia', *The Philosophical Quarterly*.

JAMES, W. (1909). 'The Dilemma of Determinism', in *The Will to Believe and Other Essays*. Cambridge, MA, Harvard University Press.

KANDEL, E. R. R., SCHWARTZ, J. H. and JESSELL, T. M. (1991). *Principles of Neural Science*. New York, Prentice Hall.

KANE, R. (1985). *Free Will and Values*. New York, State University of New York Press.

—— (1995). 'Two Kinds of Incompatibilism', in T. O'Connor, 1995a.

—— (1996). *The Significance of Free Will*. New York, Oxford University Press.

—— (1999). 'New Directions on Free Will', *Proceedings of the 20th World Congress of Philosophy*. Boston, Boston University Press.

—— (2000). 'Precis of *The Significance of Free Will*'. *Philosophy and Phenomenological Research*.

—— (2002a). *The Oxford Handbook of Free Will*. New York and Oxford, Oxford University Press.

—— (2002b). 'Some Neglected Pathways in the Free Will Debate', in Kane 2002a.

—— (2002c). 'Reflections on Free Will, Determinism and Indeterminism', The Determinism and Free Will Philosophy Website. www.ucl.ac.uk/~uctytho/dfwIntroIndex.htm

—— (2002d). 'Free Will, Determinism and Indeterminism', Proceedings of Workshop on Determinism, Ringberg Castle.

KANT, I. (1949 [1788]). *Critique of Practical Reason*, trans. L. W. Beck. Chicago, University of Chicago Press.

—— (1950 [1781]). *Critique of Pure Reason*, trans. N. Kemp Smith. London, Macmillan.

KENNY, A. (1963). *Action, Emotion and Will*. London, Routledge and Kegan Paul.

KENNY, A. (1975). *Will, Freedom and Power*. Oxford, Blackwell.

—— (1978). *Free Will and Responsibility*. London, Routledge and Kegan Paul.

KLEIN, M. (1990). *Determinism, Blameworthiness, and Deprivation*. Oxford, Oxford University Press.

KUFFLER, S. W., NICHOLLS J. G., and MARTIN, A. R. (1984) *From Neuron to Brain*. Sunderland, MA, Sinauer.

LACEY, N. (1988). *State Punishment*. London, Routledge.

LEHRER, K. (ed.) (1966). *Freedom and Determinism*. New York, Random House.

—— (1997). *Self Trust: A Study of Reason, Knowledge and Autonomy*. Oxford, Clarendon Press.

LEWIS, D. (1986). *On the Plurality of Worlds*. Oxford, Blackwell.

LUCAS, J. R. (1962). 'Causation', in *Analytical Philosophy*, 1st Series, ed. R. J. Butler. Oxford, Blackwell.

—— (1967). 'Freedom and Prediction', *Supplementary Proceedings of the Aristotelian Society*.

LYCAN, W. (1987). *Consciousness*. Cambridge, MA, MIT Press.

MACINTYRE, A. (1971). *Against the Self-Images of the Age*. London, Duckworth.

MACKIE, J. L. (1974) *The Cement of the Universe: A Study of Causation*. Oxford, Clarendon Press.

MAGILL, K. (1997). *Freedom and Experience*. London, Macmillan; New York, St Martin's.

—— (1998). 'The Idea of a Justification of Punishment', *Critical Review of International Social and Political Philosophy*.

McFEE, G. (2000). *Free Will*. Teddington, Acumen.

McGINN, C. (1982). *The Character of Mind*. Oxford, Oxford University Press.

MELE, A. (1992). *Springs of Action: Understanding Intentional Behaviour*. Oxford, Oxford University Press.

—— (1995). *Autonomous Agents: From Self-Control to Autonomy*. New York, Oxford University Press.

—— (2002). 'Autonomy, Self-Control, and Weakness of Will', in Kane 2002a.

MELLOR, D. H. (1995). *The Facts of Causation*. London, Routledge.

MILL, J. S. (1979). *Collected Works of John Stuart Mill*, ed. J. M. Robson. Toronto, University of Toronto Press.

MOORE, G. E. (1912). *Ethics*. London, Williams and Norgate.

MORGENBESSER, S. and WALSH, J. (1962). *Free Will*. Englewood Cliffs, NJ, Prentice Hall.

NAGEL, T. (1979). 'Moral Luck', in his *Mortal Questions*. Cambridge, Cambridge University Press.

—— (1986). *The View From Nowhere*. New York, Oxford University Press.

NINO, C. (1983). 'A Consensual Theory of Punishment', *Philosophy and Public Affairs*.

NOZICK, R. (1970). 'Newcomb's Problem and Two Principles of Choice', in *Essays in Honor of Carl G. Hempel*, ed. N. Rescher et al. Dordrecht, Reidel.

—— (1981). *Philosophical Explanations*. Oxford, Oxford University Press.

O'CONNOR, D. J. (1971). *Free Will*. Garden City, Anchor.

O'CONNOR, T. (ed.) (1995a). *Agents, Causes, Events: Essays on Indeterminism and Free Will*. New York, Oxford University Press.

—— (1995b). 'Agent Causation', in O'Connor 1995a.

—— (2000). *Persons and Causes: The Metaphysics of Free Will*. New York, Oxford University Press.

—— (2002). 'Libertarian Views: Dualist and Agent-Causal Theories', in Kane 2002a.

OMNES, R. (1994). *The Interpretation of Quantum Mechanics*. Princeton, Princeton University Press.

O'SHAUGHNESSY, B. (1980). *The Will*. Cambridge, Cambridge University Press.

PAGELS, H. R. (1983). *The Cosmic Code: Quantum Physics as the Language of Nature*. New York, Simon and Schuster.

PAPINEAU, D. (2000). *Introducing Consciousness*. Cambridge and New York, Totem Books.

PARFIT, D. (1984). *Reasons and Persons*. Oxford, Oxford University Press.

PEARS, D. (1963). *Freedom and the Will*. London, Macmillan.

PENROSE, R. (1989). *The Emperor's New Mind*. Oxford, Oxford University Press.

—— (1994). *Shadows of the Mind*. Oxford, Oxford University Press.

PEREBOOM, D. (1995). 'Determinism al Dente', *Nous*.

—— (2000). 'Alternate Possibilities and Causal Histories', *Philosophical Perspectives*.

—— (2001). *Living Without Free Will*. Cambridge, Cambridge University Press.

—— (2002). 'Living Without Free Will: The Case for Hard Compatibilism', in Kane 2002a.

PRIEST, S. (1991). *Theories of the Mind*. London, Penguin.

PUTNAM, H. (1975). 'The Meaning of "Meaning"', in his *Mind, Language and Reality*, vol. 2. Cambridge, Cambridge University Press.

RAWLS, J. (1971). *A Theory of Justice*. Oxford, Oxford University Press.

REID, T. (1969 [1788]). *Essays on the Active Powers of the Human Mind*, ed. Baruch Brody. Cambridge, MA, MIT Press.

ROWE, W. L. (1995). 'Two Concepts of Freedom', in O'Connor 1995a.

RUSSELL, B. (1917). *Mysticism and Logic*. London, Allen and Unwin

RUSSELL, P. (1995). *Freedom and Moral Sentiments*. New York, Oxford University Press.

SARTRE, J.-P. (1943). *Being and Nothingness*, trans. Hazel Barnes. London, Methuen.

SCHLESINGER, G. (1974). 'The Unpredictability of Free Choices', *British Journal for the Philosophy of Science*.

—— (1976). 'An Important Difference Between People and Mindless Machines', *American Philosophical Quarterly*.

SCHOPENHAUER, A. (1999). *Prize Essay on the Freedom of the Will*, trans. E. F. J. Payne, ed. Gunter Zoller. Cambridge, Cambridge University Press.

SEARLE, J. (1980). 'Minds, Brains and Programs', *Behavioral and Brain Sciences*.

—— (1983). *Intentionality*. Cambridge, Cambridge University Press.

—— (1992). *The Rediscovery of the Mind*. Cambridge, MA, and London, MIT Press.

—— (2000). 'Consciousness, Free Action and the Brain', *Journal of Consciousness Studies*.

SHER, G. (1987). *Desert*. Princeton, Princeton University Press.

SHOEMAKER, S. (1981). 'Some Varieties of Functionalism', in his *Identity, Cause and Mind*. Cambridge, Cambridge University Press.

SMILANSKY, S. (1993). 'Does the Free Will Debate Rest on a Mistake?', *Philosophical Papers*.

—— (1997). 'Can a Determinist Help Herself?', in C. H. Manekin and M. Kellner, *Freedom and Moral Responsibility: General and Jewish Perspectives*. College Park MD, University of Maryland Press.

—— (2000). *Free Will and Illusion*. Oxford, Oxford University Press.

SNYDER, A. A. (1972). 'The Paradox of Determinism', *American Philosophical Quarterly*.

SOSA, E. and TOOLEY, M. (eds) (1993). *Causation*. Oxford, Oxford University Press.

SPRIGGE, T. (1983). *The Vindication of Absolute Idealism*. Edinburgh, Edinburgh University Press.

SQUIRES, E. (1994). *The Mystery of the Quantum World*. Bristol and Philadelphia, Institute of Physics Publishing.

STICH, S. (1981). 'On the Relation Between Occurrents and Contentful Mental States', *Inquiry.*

STRAWSON, G. (1986). *Freedom and Belief.* Oxford, Clarendon Press.

—— (1995). 'Libertarianism, Action and Self-Determination', in O'Connor 1995a.

—— (1998). 'Free Will', in Craig 1998.

—— (2000). 'The Unhelpfulness of Indeterminism', *Philosophy and Phenomenological Research.*

STRAWSON, P. F. (1968). 'Freedom and Resentment', in his *Studies in the Philosophy of Thought and Action.* Oxford, Oxford University Press.

SUPPES, P. (1970). *A Probabilistic Theory of Causality.* Amsterdam, North Holland.

THORP, J. (1980). *Freewill: A Defence against Neurophysiological Determinism.* London, Routledge.

TRUSTED, J. (1984). *Free Will and Responsibility.* Oxford, Oxford University Press.

VAN FRASSEN, B. (1991). *Quantum Mechanics: An Empiricist View.* Oxford, Clarendon Press.

VAN INWAGEN, P. (1974). 'A Formal Approach to the Problem of Free Will and Determinism', *Theoria.*

—— (1975). 'The Incompatibility of Free Will and Determinism', *Philosophical Studies.*

—— (1983). *An Essay on Free Will.* Oxford, Oxford University Press.

—— (1989). 'When Is the Will Free?', *Philosophical Perspectives*, vol. 3, ed. J. Tomberlin. Atascadero CA, Ridgeview.

—— (2002). 'Free Will Remains a Mystery', in Kane 2002a.

WARNER, R. and SZUBKA, T. (1994). *The Mind–Body Problem: A Guide to the Current Debate.* Oxford, Blackwell.

WATSON, G. (ed.) (1982). *Free Will.* Oxford, Oxford University Press.

—— (1987). 'Free Action and Free Will', *Mind.*

WEATHERFORD, R. (1982). *The Philosophical Foundations of Probability Theory.* London, Routledge.

—— (1991). *The Implications of Determinism.* London, Routledge.

WIGGINS, D. (1970). 'Freedom, Knowledge, Belief and Causality', in *Knowledge and Necessity*, Royal Institute of Philosophy Lectures. Cambridge, Cambridge University Press.

WOLF, S. (1990). *Freedom within Reason.* Oxford, Oxford University Press.

Index